SEX IN THE CITY

LISA SUSSMAN

INDEX

CONTENTS

intro 6

1 the mating game 8

2 how to know you're good in bed 50

3 men 82

4 social intercourse 112

5 orgasm 138

6 mind your manners 172

7 getting protected 222

8 troubles in paradise 250

9 wild sex 278

10 sexionary 308

So often sex-advice books treat doing the horizontal mamba like some sort of boring washing machine manual – step one: find Part A 5 cm(2 in) from entrance to Part B; step two: hold Part C, twist 6 mm (¼ in); and so on. Sex – at least the kind that sizzles – is not about following some laid-out steps in an orderly manner. So throw away your rulers. It's time to give sex the respect it deserves.

INTRODUCTION

I wrote this book for the woman who is ready to have her sex with a cosmopolitan twist. I assume you know the basics of your body and what to do with it when you get naked with someone. I also assume that by now you have figured out that your vagina is not the only hot spot on your body for throwing an orgasm party.

After years of watching, listening – and enduring – men behaving badly, it's our turn. Think of this book as a get-together between us girls – the kind of steamy, all-out, unrestrained talk you'd have if you gathered your glossiest, smartest, sexiest, hippest single friends, poured a few drinks and let loose about dating, love and sex. Nothing is too personal, too depraved or too weird to explore, from trying to make sense of basic guy behaviour to maintaining a safe-sex fuck buddy. For instance:

• Do you know how to deal with a dating white-out?
• Have you lost your orgasm (and if so, do you know how to find it)?
• Do you know how to tell if he has a toxic penis?

So whether you are a singleton working the dating scene in a city metropolis or looking for love among the local talent in an out-of-town playing field, get ready to have your sexual consciousness raised – and (because you know how crazy insane the whole sex scene can be) laugh your head off.

CHAPTER ONE THE MATING GAME OR 'WHERE ARE ALL THE ALPHA MALES?'

Men who have **pierced** ears are better prepared for a relationship. They have experienced **pain** and they have bought **jewellery**.

WE'RE STAYING SINGLE LONGER AND GETTING DIVORCED EARLIER. BUT IF THERE ARE SO MANY SINGLE MEN AROUND, WHY CAN'T YOU GET A DATE?

FINE-TUNE YOUR RADAR

Loser-proof your life by sizing up a man in one date or less (be sure to check out the Sexionary on pages 308–20 for detailed definitions).

Freaks

- He says you remind him of his **mother**. Tempting because he'll watch chick flicks with you, but back slowly toward the door, carefully turn the handle and run like hell.
- **Confirmed lads** – do you want to waste time on a guy who crushes beer cans against his head?
- The **Prince Charming** who wants to move in after a few dates and seems to have lots of time. Unless you're a **Makeover Queen**, check his job status – chances are he can't afford his own place.
- Any guy who claims to be **Backed Up** (he's just interested in you as a place to release and dump).
- **Crotch Tweakers** – they're the only jewels you'll ever see and he's going to hog them for himself.
- **E-Males** – great for long-distance relationships, but not such a match when you need horizontal boogying.
- **Morning Afters** – they look bad when you're sober and even worse when you have a hangover.

- **IJAs** (he'll be dividing orgasms).
- Any guy with a **PG Rating**. He's gorgeous, hip on the pop-culture front, dresser extraordinaire, and – rapture! – keen on shopping with you. But you deserve more than a partner to watch *Will and Grace* with.
- **Mascara Men** (have your period and he's out the door permanently).
- **Prophets** (unless you don't mind putting your fur wrap in storage).
- **Trendoids** – fashionable belts, cool shoes... What more could you ask for in a man? Only problem is he'd rather shop at Prada than have sex.
- The **Man-Boy** loves to do wild, crazy things like whisk you away mid-week for a romantic tryst. He'll excite you with his boyish charm – for about two months. Then you'll be irritated by his zero responsibility (spot him via stock phrases like 'all righty' and 'you got it', which he uses even when you ask a serious question like, 'Could you get an AIDS test?').
- Any man who talks about his ex-girlfriend – **longingly**.

Creeps

- He asks you to **lunch** instead of dinner – he's either married or not all that interested.
- He says, 'I'm **not looking to get serious**.' Translation: He's looking for sex. And saying this means he doesn't have to worry about how you feel because, in his mind, he is being truthful.
- He says he's **too good for you**. Make him happy and believe him.
- When you get together for your first date, he tries to **shove his tongue** down your throat as a hello peck. This is not seductive.
- **Eurocreeps** – guaranteed: he'll dump you for someone younger, prettier and more successful.
- He **blanks** on your name while you're both naked.
- **Computer Men** (they're obsolete in six months' time).
- When you meet, he offers you **suggestively named** drinks.

- **Deceptionists** (once he shows his true self – in about three months – you'll: **1.** wonder what you ever had in common, **2.** get angry that you wasted so much time on him, or **3.** waste even more time trying to ferret out what were the lies and what was the truth).
- **Pig Pecker Man** (the more you take care of him, the less interested he's going to be).
- He whines at the crucial moment, 'Do we **really need** to use a condom? I really hate them!'
- **MBD** – Married But Dating (well, it's obvious, isn't it?).
- Anyone in **prison**.
- **Tweenies** – okay, so he may be a walking chemistry set of sexiness, but he still has the mentality of a 13-year-old boy.
- **Retro-Dates** and **Soul Mates** – yes, he really was that bad. Unless you want to give The Toad Defence to your friends, stop now.
- You discover the collection of Big Jugs **porno mags** next to his bed (the only thing worse is if the pages are all stuck together).

Freelancers

- He has **trouble ordering an entrée** at the restaurant (or even picking a restaurant) and figuring out if he wants to walk or take a cab. This guy buckles under the weight of making any decision – including whether he wants a full-time girlfriend or a casual relationship.

- He **channel-surfs** nonstop. It means he's convinced that there is always something better out there – an attitude he may also apply to his relationships (so be prepared for lots of babe gawking).

- Someone who does a **Fade Out**. Perhaps he had meningitis, but more likely he was hunting around to see if he could find a better deal and, after a few expeditions, realized you were worth more than he initially thought. So he plays dumb and calls (this is no guarantee he won't go shopping again).

- Every woman you meet when you are out together seems to know him… **intimately**.

- **Himbos**. Sigh. Those muscles. But all the hours he spends at the gym bulking up, not to mention the hours spent gazing at his reflection in the mirror, in store windows, on the back of his spoon can make a girl feel lonely. Not to mention that the only person he's into having a long-term relationship with is himself.

- **Male Sluts** – just do it for the sex.

TIP If you don't care that they're not long lasting but wouldn't mind a little horizontal hustle, freelancers can make good Fuck Buddies. Just keep it simple – if either of you starts having sex with someone else, the Law of Relativity kicks in.

THE UNTOUCHABLES

Certain guys are off limits for a one-night stand, a cheat or **anything more than a drink** in a crowded place.

- His **best friend**
- Any **close member** of his family
- Your **boss's** significant other
- Your **sister's** boyfriend/husband
- A **casual friend's** or co-worker's ex (let there be at least one person between you or you will be seen as the Other Woman)
- A **friend's** Fuck Buddy
- Your **best friend's** boyfriend/crush

THE AGE GAP

The highs and lows of going out with someone a different age.

TOY BOY VS ANTIQUING

TOY BOY	ANTIQUING
Men under 25 are not relationship material – they are, at best, a fetish.	Men over 55 are relationship material – if you have a father complex.
He'll come in seconds flat.	The older he gets, the longer he lasts.
On the other hand, he'll be hard again and again and again in seconds flat.	Although erections are slower to come, he makes up in quality for what he may lack in quantity.
He may think that a clitoris is a rare Amazonian flower.	You do not have to explain the importance of the clitoris to him or how women reach orgasm.
He's fit, lithe and full of life (but, yes, face it, a bit pimply).	He's a bit saggy.
You're diving into a pool of men who are virtually baggage free. Chances are there are no issues with children or child support, and no alimony payments.	He doesn't live with his parents.
He cuts his hair short instead of combing it over.	He'll be able to plan his weekends without the constant need to check out what his 'buddies' are doing.
You'll always be older than him.	You'll always be younger than him.
He probably doesn't have much of a career at this stage.	He's financially secure.
He still thinks Pamela Anderson was born that way.	He's going to be deeply appreciative of your 'young' body.
He's too young to be neurotic yet, and too naive to see how neurotic you are.	He's been through it all and is now emotionally stable.

TIP Age differences are like dog years. There may be only ten years between the two of you, but in reality it's probably about seventy.

Best bet Stick with someone within plus or minus five years of your own age.

Lust busts

If it's been awhile since your **last orgasm**, it can be hard to make a rational judgment about a guy. If any of the following apply, you may just be worried that you'll **never have sex again**.

- You're out with him and you are overcome with an urgent need to know what's happening on your least favourite soap.
- You're bored even when *you* talk.
- You experience **Deja Moo**.
- You flirt with the waiter, the man having dinner with his wife at the next table, the doorman.
- You start glazing over.

- You notice **little things** – the printer's credit on the bottom of the menu; the way the little hairs on the back of your hand go one way, then the other way; the blonde-to-brunette ratio in the room.
- You think it can't be this bad, so something must be wrong with you. (No, it really is this bad.)
- Employ the **Law of Relativity**: how attractive your ex appears to be is directly proportionate to how unattractive your date is.
- You feel you are soul mates the moment you meet – it might be Love At First Sight Disorder.

- He says, **'I don't want to just rush into sex.'** It's tempting to translate this as the ultimate put-down and decide you will do everything and anything to make him want you. But ruling out brain damage and virginity, a man who says this generally means: **1.** he only finds you semi-appealing but wants to keep you on the just-in-case-he-has-nothing-else-going-on backburner, **2.** he's gay but doesn't realize it, or **3.** he has an STI/STD or is impotent and doesn't know how to tell you about it yet. Of course, he could just be an incredibly sweet guy who digs your company and realizes the first time will be better if there's some anticipation. But you'll only realize that after you break up with him.

Should you have sex tonight?

RATING

❤ : Use your hand instead.

❤❤ : A quick snog in the back of the car will have the same effect.

❤❤❤ : Go for it.

1. It's this or eating a box of chocolates. ❤
2. You can't sleep. ❤
3. There's absolutely nothing to watch on TV. ❤
4. You want to get back at your ex. ❤❤
5. You haven't had sex in ages and you've just got to get back on that horse (and let's hope your next fling is hung like one, honey). ❤❤❤
6. You want to snag him. ❤❤❤ (This is not a guaranteed success.)
7. You've just come out of a long line of long-term relationships. ❤❤❤
8. You're tired of the hassles of serious commitments. ❤❤❤

Now, how to **make sure** he knows what you know so he **won't** call again.

1. Tell him about your ex, who left you at the altar. He's still sticking around? Then...

2. Go on and on about the amount of therapy it's taken for you to get to a 'forgiving place'. He's still calling?

3. Add how your father will never let you forget how much money he blew on the non-reception and how he is determined to vet any potentially serious boyfriends. Not scared off yet?

4. Mention how your mother is desperate to see you married with children. In the unlikely event that he has not left town without a forwarding number...

5. Let drop how your ex had a restraining order put out on you for stalking (add a disclaimer here that you were just out walking your cat).

If he still **seems interested**, it's time for **drastic** measures: tell him that you always follow your horoscope's advice, and this morning yours said that you should stay celibate for six months to clear out all the **evil demons.** Guaranteed: he'll be calling for the bill before you've finished your spiel.

THE MEET MARKET

Guys think that they have to do all the hard work – walk up to the woman, make her laugh and ask her out. If they only knew all the blood, sweat and tears that the woman has put into making herself look fabulous, appearing approachable and locating a man-friendly place. Face it: if you want to lose that **Born-Again Virgin** feeling, you've got to shop till you drop.

PLOY 1: **WEAR THE RIGHT SEXESSORIES**

Carry a camcorder.

It's choice for scooping a guy out, analysing him with your friends post-date and incorporating into your sex-play later.

Get online.

Start a web page announcing the up-to-the-second status of relationships so you can easily find out when the hooked-up eye candy you've been salivating over is about to launch out on his own.

Start a recycling (men) programme.

Throw a 'leftover guy' party. Ask your friends to bring along their dishiest 'leftover guy' and some food – something sexy like oysters or chocolate.

Hunt down a big, friendly, drooling hound.

Instant guy magnets. Clearly, since you don't have one of your own, you will have to borrow – offer to pet-sit for friends or family (just hide all your Manolos first).

Wear other men on your arm.

It makes guys wonder why you're such a honey trap, and all that testosterone sends your flirty side soaring.

Hold a one-woman wet T-shirt contest.

Wait for a rainstorm, then slip into a skimpy shirt and put yourself in the vicinity of a hunky guy – you're giving him all the incentive he needs to approach.

Carry your breasts with you at all times.

Reaching by him for something with a slight (or firm) brush of your breast, as though it's unintentional, works at many levels. Maybe it *is* unintentional. But he'd rather think it's your way of saying you want to go to bed with him NOW.

Pretend to sprain your ankle.

All men love to fix things and your faux injury will appeal to his inner surgeon.

Change your job.

These are the professions with the most sex appeal: masseuse, flight attendant, cocktail waitress, nurse and Playboy bunny. So, the choice is yours...

TIP Lose your friends. It used to be popular to go trolling with a posse. But the drawbacks are many: 1. you may all want the same eye candy, 2. they may get him, 3. if they don't, they may do a Data Dump, and 4. he will have to cross no-man's land first.

INSIDER TIP Forget the leather pants. Yeah, they look hot but you might end up failing the Sniff Test (see page 176).

PLOY 2: **KNOW YOUR LINES**

- 'Hi, my name is...'

- 'Let's grab a beer.'

- Touch his watch and ask,
  'Do you have the time?'

- 'Do you have a girlfriend/boyfriend?'

- If there's been a lot of eye contact,
  approach and say, 'So, are we going out
  or what?'

- Slip a note with your phone number
  on it into his pocket.

- Tell him you're a lesbian.

- 'Wanna have sex?' (Variation: 'I want
  to have sex with you.')

PLOY 3: **MEET AND GREETS**

Had it with the bar and party scene? Here's a few
ways to work the **Foreign Market**.

- **Crash a funeral.**
  Grieving widowers are easy targets – but you have
  to be prepared to end up a **Decoy**.

- **Hit on the latest horror flick.**
  Apparently, getting the willies scared out of them puts
  guys in the mood. So does listening to a Steve Martin
  comedy routine. Go figure.

- **Trawl your supermarket.**
  The timing is more important than what's in your trolley.
  You need to go between 7.30 and 9.00 am on a Sunday.
  Of course, you may not want to be with someone who
  spends valuable weekend snooze-time squeezing melons.

    - **Join a cult.**
      Try to find the type that celebrates with mass marriages
      rather than mass suicide pacts.

    - **Go to Emergency.**
      Hold out for a doctor – if he is on call, he will be short of
      sleep and have lowered defences.

    - **Scope out a convention.**
      It's a prime place to meet lots of men who aren't pissed.
      (Unless you speak Romulan, avoid Trekkie conventions.)

- **Go on a blind date.**

  It will make your mother happy and, anyway, arranged marriages seem to work.

- **Try speed dating.**

  Billed as an alternative to blind dates, these events for marriage-minded men and women to evaluate potential are now held regularly around the world. A group of single men and woman gather together in one place to meet and mingle, following a strict time-schedule and specific rules. Each pair gets 7 minutes to chat before both partners must move on to the next 'date' (usually eight in one night). During this time you can ask your partner anything except his or her age, occupation and place of residence. The idea is to focus on what the person is *really* like. When the bell rings, regardless of how engrossing the conversation, you move on. At evening's end, participants indicate on a card which (if any!) of their partners appealed to them enough to go out on a less speedy date. If there's a match, the man is given the woman's phone number.

  - **Or online personals.**

    Be prepared for lots of Before-Play. Think about it – you're planning to pad *your* résumé, aren't you? The key is to be honest enough yourself so you don't have to explain how you gave up mountain climbing in the hour you spent travelling to meet him, and suspicious enough of him that you don't meet him alone or in an unknown place.

Advertising yourself

Contrary to what most people think, writing a personal ad is **NOT** an act of desperation. It just means you finally admitted – or figured out – that you can't tell if you're going to get along with someone just from what he looks like in a dark bar. Nobody can.

Personal ads help filter out the losers. The important thing is not to be cheap. Pay for extra words to make sure you **give a clear picture** of yourself. Better yet, include a photo. A recent, representative one. It'll get you more responses, no matter what you look like: people just want to be reassured that you don't have two heads.

Be specific. Otherwise you'll end up wasting a lot of time on men you have nothing in common with. Don't just say you like movies (who doesn't like movies? – but his idea of a great flick could be *Debbie Does Dallas*). Mention what kind of movies you like – titles, types, stars. Same goes for sense of humour – who doesn't want someone who can laugh? But there's a huge difference between Monty Python-funny and Benny Hill-funny.

At the same time, avoid TMI. There is such a thing as **Too Much Information**. Do people really need to know that your last boyfriend found your breasts too large? Save something for later. Avoid mentioning exes, your dietary likes and similar.

It helps to visit any other personals website. Read a handful of profiles. Note what seems like cheese to you and make sure you **don't add to the fromage**.

Also, don't be afraid to be honest about what you want – personals let you **cut through all the bullshit** much faster.

Don't like something (insert pet peeve/body type/mental disorder)? Then say so in your ad and weed out the undesirables. If he has to be a professional, say so. Same goes for the rest: religion, age range you can live with, salary you can live with, previous (or current) marriage status (does it matter if he's never been married, is still married, is in the middle of a messy divorce?). Do you want kids, do you mind if he has them? Do you care if he uses drugs/smokes/teetotals? Consider his sleep habits (you don't want a morning person chirpily offering you a glass of OJ if you're a night owl), political leanings, address (do you want the hassle of a long-distance relationship?), interests and musical tastes. But **be realistic**. Don't ask for a 1.9 m (6 ft 2 in) man who's intelligent, gorgeous, successful, unencumbered and looking for a relationship – unless you want someone as seriously self-delusional as you appear to be.

When replying

- Proof and spellcheck. It's the least you can do.
- Don't use a form letter. It's obvious and makes them feel you couldn't care less.
- Include a question – it creates dialogue (and 'what's your favourite number?' does not count).
- Give them space. Don't stalk them if they don't respond immediately. After one witty follow-up and still no response, pull the plug.
- No me-me-me-logues. The first response you send is not an opportunity to tell your life story.

The more specific you are, the better your chance of success. If this seems like too much work, stick to the bars.

Are you dating yet?

In San Francisco, the courts have done something that the rest of us have been unable to do since the very first caveman bagged a wife – define dating. Apparently, a dating relationship is in fact 'a social relationship between two individuals who have a reciprocally amorous and increasingly exclusive interest in one another, and shared expectation of the growth of that mutual interest, that has endured for such a length of time and stimulated frequent interactions that the relationship cannot be deemed to have been casual.'

Back right up – a dating relationship? For the rest of us, dating is what you do **BEFORE** the relationship – the try before you buy. It's the last look at yourself in the mirror from behind in a new cocktail dress before you hand over your credit card to the cashier and make a commitment. In other words, dating is, 'Want to grab a coffee?' not 'Want to exchange keys?'

But just in case, here's how to talk the talk while **you do the walk**.

'We're just friends.'

You hang out, you have things in common, you have swapped stories but not tongues – yet. You now need to get really drunk together.

'We're dating.'

All of the above but now you have swapped tongues and probably other parts of your body, but you are not exclusive (at least he isn't).

'We're getting serious.'

You've had The Talk, agreed not to see anyone else and know what you are doing on the weekends. Baby-talk is optional at this stage.

'We're a couple.'

You didn't have sex last Saturday night, despite having rented one of your favourite chick flicks.

New lounge rules

What is the one thing that all men at singles bars have in common? They're married.

Step-by-step bar etiquette

1. **Walk to the beat.** If there's music on, it will catch his eye.

2. **Brandish a beer bottle.** It sends the signal that you're the kind of girl he can be himself around (not to mention the subliminal message he'll get watching you wrap your lips around a long, cylindrical object).

3. **Call in a substitute.** Flirting with his friends triggers a sense of rivalry in the guy you're after, forcing him to find a way into the conversation and exclude his buddy (never underestimate the competition between men).

4. **Make him feel protective.** Put him on guard duty by dropping your sweater or jacket down on the bar and saying, 'Can you do me a massive favour and watch this for a second? I have to run to the ladies' room.' Alternatively, walk up and say, 'Could I talk to you for a couple of minutes? There's someone I'm trying to avoid.'

5. **Make him feel smart.** After positioning yourself next to him, order a beer, take a sip, make a face and ask him if it tastes soapy. It doesn't matter if he takes you up on your offer and tastes it. You've made the opening to say, 'I'm going to order another. Can I get you something?'

EAU DE DESPERATION

Desperation reeks, and not in that good pheromone kind of way. Here's how to look a little less like a sexual welfare case.

1. Leave yourself alone. Go easy on the make-up and perfume. The main thing to load up on is deodorant and powder.

2. Slow down. You are hitting on him harder than sledgehammer. He needs to get a move in edge-wise. And, of course, the danger of coming at him with such force is that you're more likely to let slip that you are sex frantic. In which case you may as well be flashing **LOSER** over your head. One guaranteed way to grab – and hold – his attention is to ask, 'Ever had a threesome?'

3. Don't panic. If your potential orgasm donor is making restless moves, lay your cards on the table. Say 'I'm leaving. Want to come?' Chances are he'll follow like a dog on a lead.

LAST CALL MOVE Give him the 'come-and-get-me' tap. As you pass on your way to the bar, instead of saying **'Excuse me,'** put your hand on his back. Use gentle pressure, as if he were already your lover. When he looks to see who's behind him, say, **'I'm sorry, I was just trying to get past.'** Then flash him an innocent smile and move on. He'll follow you to the ends of the earth (or at least to your apartment).

Let him **see you play** with yourself

Forget what you wear on top. Your number one must-have for turning an otherwise evolved man into a drooling, panting fool is a thong (note: no need to bare-all with a see-all outfit à la Liz Hurley – the idea is to get his imagination steaming so just let it 'accidentally' peek out from a low-slung pair of jeans). The snug fit will feel sexy against your skin and make him want to reach out for hand contact.

Once you know he's eager to touch, **drive him crazy** with a little on-the-spur masturbation. Find a stool or couch to perch on and sit with your legs crossed. Then start touching yourself where you'd like him to touch you. Caress the flesh just above your cleavage, run your hands over your hips, wriggle your bum around on the seat. You'll need to call the riot police to keep him off you.

The call back
Men don't call on weekends (that screams, 'Loser, don't you have anything better to do?'). They don't call on the hour, quarter hour, half hour or three-quarter hour (that seems too planned). They are more likely to call in the evening than the day (or you may think they don't have an important job). Wednesday and Thursday are the prime calling days*. If it's more than five days before he calls, he may be doing a Fade Out.

* Except during the football season – then it's any night when there isn't an important match.

Dating white-outs

Ease that instantly regrettable man mistake.

1

MISTAKE It's been two days and he hasn't called so you leave a tirade on his answering machine. Then he calls to tell you he had to go out of town suddenly and this is the first chance he's had to get in touch.

FIX-IT You could break into his place and erase the message. But you'd have an even harder time explaining your insane behaviour if you're caught. Just tell him you had a PMS moment and left a disaster message on his machine. Chances are he won't hear anything beyond 'PMS'.

2

MISTAKE You accidentally e-mail him a dish-it-all about the sex you had with him, which you were sending to all your girlfriends.

FIX-IT If it was good stuff, tell him he was such an amazing lover, you had to share with your (deeply envious) friends. If it was a bad report, who cares? Do you really want or need to continue with Lottery Sex?

3

MISTAKE You accidentally e-mail him a dish-it-all about the sex you had with someone else that you were sending to all your girlfriends.

FIX-IT Tell him it was a fantasy. Then tell him about the sexy dream you had about him last night...

4 MISTAKE He says he's staying home for the night. You don't believe him so you keep calling his number and hanging up, forgetting he has Caller ID.

FIX-IT Change your phone number.

5 MISTAKE You say, 'I love you' too soon and you know that's going to freak him out big time.

FIX-IT Add, '...when the bar has free chips/when ***** wins/when I go shopping and find five perfect outfits' – in other words, pretend that you said 'I love *it*' and he's the obsessed-about-saying-I-love-you jerk who misheard.

BODY HEAT

Check your temperature against the symptoms. You leave the house only to buy condoms and lube – it's lust. You leave the house to go shopping together – it's love.

Horniness

Instead of having breakfast, you masturbate. When introduced to a man – any man – you immediately wonder what it would be like to have a shower with him. You have an orgasm if your boss (aka Mole Man when you are in a more rational state of mind) touches your cheek. This usually happens about a week after your period, when you start ovulating (advice: carry your contraceptives with you).

WARNING You are highly susceptible to Love at First Sight Disorder. The best way to find relief is by taking care of yourself. Or get a Fuck Buddy.

Instant Lust

You see someone across the room and suddenly know for a fact that he is the most wonderful person on earth and definitely your true Soul Mate. This moment of deliriousness usually lasts until you actually speak to him and he says, **1.** 'I'm married', or **2.** 'If I could see you naked, I'd die happy.'

WARNING This won't turn into the real thing. It might, but you may also find that drinking every night really is a good diet.

Crush

Fantasies of ravishing him are the only thing that gets you through your day. **NO WARNING** Go for it. It's better than fantasies of finding the perfect Marc Jacobs dress on sale.

Infatuation

It feels like the real thing, smells like the real thing, talks like the real thing. Your heart palpitates, you spend hours gazing into each other's eyes, and you rip his clothes off at every opportunity. This passes the time better than watching paint dry, but keep in mind that it's mostly based on fantasy. 'No, no, no,' you say. 'This is different.' Maybe. But if he stifles yawns when you start talking about work, be prepared for **Assmosis**. **WARNING** Do not go away with him for more than one night or Assmosis may happen sooner than you expected.

Crazed

Your friends tell you he's a creep and not even all that good looking, but you still wake up every morning with his name in your head. He never calls when he says he will but you put your life on hold and spend all your time waiting by the phone just in case. If you have a date with him, you have to run to the mirror to check your mascara six times in 5 minutes because he is about to ring your doorbell.

WARNING Love has nothing to do with feeling nauseous. You are dangerously close to becoming a Bunny Boiler.

Serious Like

He seems really nice, smart, funny, successful, charming, a good lover, without hang-ups but... Just because he matches your checklist, it doesn't mean the chemistry is there. If you know you would survive if he disappeared from your life tomorrow, he may be just a facsimile of the Real Thing (still, he'll certainly do until the Real Thing comes along).

WARNING You may get **Double Bed Dread**. Love is not instant sunsets and violins, sometimes it grows on you – like a fungus. If, after three months, he feels more like a toadstool than a toad-about-to-turn-prince, dump him.

L-O-V-E

He's perfect until he isn't and you find you want to be with him anyway.

WARNING You may start hugging strangers in the street.

Is it the **real** thing?

So you've met someone who rings all your bells. **Attractive, affectionate, funny**. The sex is good, if not great. You're smitten, he seems smittened. How do you know if it's the real thing?

Travel together. Rent a car and take a 48-hour road trip. That's when the real personality shows up. On the road. In confined quarters. When both of you are uncomfortable. When the traffic sucks. That's when you find out how much you really like the guy. And how much he likes you.

Does he make the experience more tolerable or more of a pain? Are your personalities similar or is he an advance planner and you're more spur-of-the-moment? These are the times when personality quirks become royal pains and it's no longer cute when he whistles absentmindedly through his teeth. You want to squash a brick in his mouth. Travel is a real relationship accelerator – you just have to decide whether you are going to jump off the ride before you reach **maximum speed**.

SCREEN TESTS

He's testing, testing

Be prepared – from the moment he meets you, he is giving you a **Screen Test**. This is because men still have more power during the pre-dating time while women have more power once guys fall in love. So before a man becomes attached and allows you to have all that power over him, he is going to test your butt to the max. ALL men do this – nerds, players and even 'the marrying kind'. However, their tests have a different focus or intent.

Keep in mind that men are not **Makeover Queens**. They do not believe you can turn a Manizer into someone you take bring home to meet mom. Nor do they think that a potential **Bunny Boiler** can ever get enough therapy to be a worthwhile mate. About the only conversion he is willing to spend time on is if you are a lesbian, part-time or otherwise – mainly because his fantasy is less to change your taste to man-only than to elbow his way into the action.

Most men will give one of two generic tests, both designed to find out if they can dazzle you with their BS.

Love Terrorist

If he's a potential Love Terrorist, he wants to see how much abuse you'll take just to have him around. So he'll try to find out **how needy and weak** you are, your level of self-esteem, what your expectations are about the men in your life (do they need to tell the truth for you to be with them? can they sleep with your best friend without you breaking it off?) and how easily he can twist you around his finger (in his mind, a metaphor for his penis). His tests will mainly be focused on what's wrong with you (you insist on knowing his last name, you won't have sex with him before you know his last name, you don't believe that he can't give out his last name because he is an international spy).

Here are some of his words/actions and their **hidden meanings**.

'I think I'm really beginning to have feelings for you – I hope that's okay.'
He doesn't say what those feelings are – they may be, 'You're starting to grate on my nerves' or, more likely, horniness. He's throwing out some bait to trap you into revealing your thoughts and feelings about what's going on.

He says, 'I think I love you' (or some variation of) within a week of meeting.
He is trying to find out how much of a sucker you are.

He constantly shows up late or not at all.
He wants to know how much bad behaviour you will tolerate.

He promises to whisk you off for a five-star vacation somewhere expensive and romantic.
He is trying to find out how important his wallet is to you.

He says he is married, living with someone or has a girlfriend but that they have an 'understanding'/ he is unhappy and can't leave her because she might commit suicide/he is planning to end it as soon as he finds the right moment.
He is trying to find out if you will tolerate a Free Market.

Commitment Man

A man looking for **wife material** has made the decision
that he's ready to settle down and now his main goal is to
find someone to do it with – fast.

He wants to be extraordinarily sure that you are the
woman he needs in his life before he commits himself and
opens up his heart, home and wallet. So he will test you to
find out whether you will trick or betray him, your nagging
style, how you feel about children and what you look like
naked (really naked, without make-up, teeth brushed, hair
washed – the way he figures it, he is going to be seeing
you in every situation and he doesn't want any erection-
meltdown surprises like discovering you have Millennium
Domes). He will also test your mother – he wants to know
how well you are going to hold up in 30 years' time.

Here are some of the ploys a man
interested in **commitment** will try
and how to read them.

**He invites you on a date that
includes spending time with
the under-five set.**
He wants to know how you do
on the nurturing mama front.

He asks you to come out with his crew and they then start busting his balls.

He is trying to find out how loyal you are and whether you will support him or join in if the going gets tough.

He asks you to come out again with his crew.

He wants to see if you understand these are *his* friends and not yours and that you are expected to maintain a certain distance with them.

He gives you the drunk test.

He takes you out clubbing, buys you plenty to drink, and then pretends he is sick and has to go home but urges you to stay. If you insist on going home with him, you pass. If you agree to stay he'll pretend to leave, then lurk around (or get a friend to) to see how you behave.

He talks about cheating – maybe how a friend got cheated on, or his ex-woman cheated on him.

He wants to know your stance on fidelity in relationships.

He double-checks, getting his best friend to hit on you.

He wants to know whether you'll stay loyal in the heat of the moment.

And you're just **checking**

Sure, his **mouth is like fire** but if more than three of the
following apply, it's time to call a **Code Blue** on
the relationship.

1. He doesn't want commitment and you do.
2. He wants commitment and you don't.
3. He's done a **Bit Flip**.
4. He's more an Er-hem than a boyfriend.
5. He lives with his mother, (supposedly) ex-girlfriend/
   cocktail waitress/wannabe model/'cousin'.
6. He believes in the **Law of the Jungle**.
7. He's MBD, a Male Slut and/or Therapeutically Correct.
8. He forgets your name, address, mobile/home phone
   numbers between oral baths.
9. The only shoes he owns are trainers.

Directional signals

How to know if he is **straight-straight**, **gay-straight** or **straight gay**.

The Stereotypical Neatness Test

If his shirts are ironed and tucked in properly, his socks match his shirt, his hair is neatly trimmed, his bed is made and there's very little dirty laundry on the kitchen floor, **he may be gay** or he may just live with his mother (which doesn't really rule out that he's gay). **BUT** if there isn't a significant amount of dirt under at least two or three of his fingernails, there is a very good chance he's either gay-straight or straight gay.

The Seduction Test

Show him your breasts. If he doesn't react, **he's straight gay or a very smart straight-straight** who is hoping you'll reveal even more in your quest for knowledge.

If he scored...

below 10 points

He's straight-straight (good to sleep with but keep girlfriends on call for everything else).

between 10 and 15 points

He's gay-straight (a great boyfriend – but don't expect any sparks to fly when you do the horizontal mamba).

above 15 points

He's straight gay (you can shop with him, cuddle up to him at night, call all hours without him feeling suffocated – in short, he's the perfect boyfriend if you own a vibrator).

Give him the GAT (Gay Aptitude Test)

5 points if he wears a polo- (turtle-) neck sweater year-round

5 points if he eats yoghurt more than twice a week

1 point for every plant he has in the house, excluding marijuana and fly traps

3 points for every plant he's named

1 point for every poster or picture framed in his room

5 points for every poster of a musical or play

1 point for every skin-care product he owns

5 points if he has a padded toilet-seat cover

5 points if he has shag carpet on the lid of the toilet

5 points if he drinks white wine spritzers

5 points if he has potpourri in his bathroom

1 point for potpourri in any other room

3 points if he wraps gifts himself – beautifully

5 points if he has stationery

25 points if he has a squeegee in the shower

And finally, give him...

50 points if he's ever blown a guy.

How to claw your way out of Heartbreak Hell

There's more to it than eating ice-cream (although that has been shown to help in some cases). **Here's how to feel better in one month or less.**

- **Go as low as you can.** Call your break-up recovery team. Get drunk on bad red wine. Play Country and Western music (it'll help put your pain in perspective).

- **Get laid.** Call a Freelancer friend and feel desired.

- **Get creative.** Instead of wasting your time driving by his house ten times a day to see if his car is there, do all those things you have been putting off since your relationship began.

- **Do not call your ex.** Right now you need to go cold turkey. Instead, call your Freelancer friend again.

- **Go ahead and get revenge.** But get the smart kind, not the kind that lands you in jail. Instead of stalking him, stalk your gym. He always wanted you to try some new sexual move? Do it with your Freelancer friend (if you want, you can make sure it gets back to your ex). In other words, do things that will help you more than they will hurt him.

- **Do not remember the good times.** Instead, remind yourself of every fault he had, from selfishly eating the last spoonful of ice-cream to brown-nosing his boss.

- **Go shopping.** To hell with your budget – you can balance your chequebook next month. Buy some fabulous lingerie and then call your Freelancer friend to rip it off.

ONE LAST FABULOUS SUM-IT-UP TIP Don't worry if your step-in guy is gay – a gay man will tell you if the shirt colour works, if you have olive bits stuck in your teeth and if another guy really *is* hot or if it's just that he dresses well.

CHAPTER TWO HOW TO KNOW YOU'RE GOOD IN BED OR 'WAS IT GOOD FOR ME?'

2

Why don't women **blink** during foreplay? They don't have **time**.

FORGET KNOCKING YOUR SOCKS OFF. HERE'S HOW TO SEND YOUR ENTIRE WARDROBE FLYING, GET READY TO SQUIRM WITH SATISFACTION AND LEAVE HIM GROVELLING BY THE BED.

BEG-FOR-MERCY
MANOEUVRES

Bustiers and sensual massages can only take you so far.
Sure, doing it upside-down hanging from a chandelier clad
in nothing but garters is going to drive you both into a hot
lusty frenzy once. But it's technique that keeps you coming
– and coming back for more.

However, while men and women aren't from different
planets, simple biology confirms that we are not made on
the same basic model. So what gets his motor revving
might not have the same turn-on effect for you. Perfect
these his-and-her beg-for-mercy manoeuvres, and you'll
both never want to get out of bed.

He can

1. Use a timer.

Fifteen minutes. Is that too much to ask? Just 15 little bitty
minutes of foreplay. Here's the schedule.

- **Zero to Minute 3** Mute the TV and get rid of the
  nachos. He should kiss you like you're the only thing
  in the world that exists right now.

- **Minute 3 to Minute 7** He should kiss you some
  more. But while he's doing it, he should begin to touch
  you all over. No, no. Not like that. Like this – gently, like
  your body is something he's never seen before. Now
  he should let you touch him.

- **Minute 7 to Minute 12** He should begin very, very slowly to take off your clothes. And he can start to take off his and let you finish for him. Do not – do we really need to say this? yes, we do – FOLD anything.

- **Minute 12 to Minute 15** It's time to use your mouth. Everywhere. Nibble, lick, bite. A little roughly on ordinary skin; a little more gently elsewhere. From head to toe and back again. Most men misread their lover's arousal signs. Getting juicy doesn't mean she's instantly ready to do the horizontal dance.

- **Drop anchor**
  Important: in future, vary the order in each time zone.

2. Use a tissue.

Why don't men ask where the clitoris is? Because they hate asking directions.The importance of understanding the clitoris can't be over-emphasized. The myth is: if you rub long enough, it will happen. It won't. Actually, direct pressure to the clitoris is very unpleasant. It's much sexier to caress the side gently.

It also helps if he knows what the following are and how to locate them (hint – they're all erogenous zones): nipple, labia major, labia minor, mons, vaginal canal and cervix.

TIP One side of your clitoris might be more sensitive — and apt to bring you more pleasure — than the other. Once you've figured out which side it is, tell him subtly by rotating your hips so his finger or mouth automatically slips into position.

3. Use his fingers.

You have to admit – the penis is an imperfect sex tool. It's too unpredictable, clumsy and pointy to use on many parts of a woman's body. But his hands have no such limitations. The best lovers are guys who know exactly what to do with those items hanging off the ends of their arms...

...on your breasts

Men treat breasts as if they were dartboards – they always aim for the bull's-eye. That's fine, but let him know he can score points anywhere on the board. Which means he should use his entire hand, and focus on the entire breast. Cupping and cuddling is especially good. Flicking nipples and gently pinching is fine. Twiddling your nipples between finger and thumb like he's trying to find a radio station in a hilly area is not.

...on your genitals

When you masturbate, you usually rest your wrist on your lower abdomen. But when he stimulates your genitals, he's forced to contort arm and hand to get the same position. Ask him to try sitting underneath you, your back against his front. He can then reach his hand around and rest his wrist just above your pubic bone.

Hopefully he won't make the mistake most guys do and rely on one finger. He needs at least two, ideally three or four. Keeping the heel of his palm on your mons, he should curl his fingers in gentle back-and-forth and circular motions between your lips and clitoris. He can start slowly, adding a little 'air time' to keep you guessing, then increase his speed as your arousal builds.

...in your genitals

The one advantage his thinner, shorter fingers have over the organ that was designed specifically to fill a vagina? Unlike his erect penis, they bend. So they can focus on a particular spot in the vagina in ways that his penis can't. Get his knuckles into the act. A come-hither motion along the upper wall of the vagina – about 2.5 cm (1 in) in – is the best. But don't let him waste time focusing all his energy in one place. It's the ring around the lower third of the vagina that has the most nerve endings.

4. Use the rest of your body.

Your body is not some highway with just three turnoffs: Breastville East and West, and the Midtown Tunnel. There are vast areas of it which he ignores far too often as he goes bombing straight into downtown Vagina. It's time for him to start paying some attention...

...to your bum

Grab it, knead, pinch, squeeze, or even lightly slap it. One thing he should keep in mind: strokes that lift or separate the cheeks are better than those that depress or bring them together.

...to your perineum

This is that little area just behind the opening of your vagina. There are a lot of nerve endings in the perineum that respond well to light pressure or gentle stroking. If he can reach it, this is an area that may be great to stimulate during thrusting. He should use one or two fingers to apply about the same amount of pressure you'd use to push an elevator button. But he needs to be careful. The perineum is close to another opening – the anus – one that should never be entered without an invitation.

...to your hips

Of all the places he can park his hands during intercourse, the hips offer one of the best. If you're on top, he can use his hands to help guide you as you thrust. It's like power steering – you're still in control but you don't have to work as hard. If he's on top, he should reach under you and use his hands to grasp your hips and lift your pelvis toward him. His thrusts will be deeper.

> ## ONE ALL-TIME TECHNIQUE FOR HIM TO MASTER
> Rubbing you the right way in a full-body erotic massage, starting at the top of your head and working his way through every nook and crevice. Minimum time: 30 minutes.

5. Use his other digit.

There is one way to make his penis do things it can't do on its own. Give it a helping hand. It can be very erotic to be teased at the opening of the vagina. He (or you) can grasp the base of his penis and gently make circles around the clitoris, or run the underside of the shaft along your inner lips. But don't penetrate.

6. Use no-doze.

Once you get going, there should be no stopping for a break. Women, unlike men, don't pick up where they left off. If he stops, you plummet back to square one.

There is no known biological reason for men to fall asleep immediately after sex. But it's not just a matter of propping eyelids open. Any woman is going to find it sexy if her partner makes sure she is as satisfied as he obviously is.

You can

1. Show yourself.

Men like to see naked women. That's why they like porn. This doesn't mean you have to slap on nipple tassels and perform a strip act. Simply leave the lights on during sex.

2. Show him your inner guy and spit on him.

Unlike women, men do not have built-in lubricants. You *can* stroke it dry, but you may as well suggest a session of carpet burns for all the pleasure it will give him. Saliva is your best lubricant, so give your hand a big sexy lick.

3. Show him that you know his body better than he knows it himself.

Many men aren't aware of the range of erotic areas on their bodies. Surprise him: instead of directing most of your attention to what's below his belt, try these...

...his ears

Poking in and out with a wet tongue makes him go crazy, especially if you breathe a little dirty talk in to the mix.

...the back of his neck

Just lightly scratching his neck using small, circular movements is extremely exciting for him.

...his nipples

These are exclamation points for him – make them shout with a little kissing and caressing. The more pressure you use, the better.

...his lower belly

This is like an oasis stop on the way down to the penis. Licking it or even tracing your finger over the area will make him stand and quiver to attention.

...his bum

As much as he likes you paying attention to the doorpull at the front, he likes your hands to wander around to the backdoor occasionally to make his thighs feel naughty and oh! sooooo nice.

4. Show that you want to make friends with his best friend.

Explore the three hot spots around his genitals...

...the frenulum

This is the place on the underside of his penis where the foreskin attaches to the head. An ultra-sensitive spot, it is like a male clitoris – packed with nerve endings. A little added pressure from your fingers and you'll set off an orgasmic chain reaction.

...the perineum

Pressing this little triangle of love nestling between his scrotum and his anus can intensify the level of his orgasms. Try using two fingers for 2 seconds, and then release. Do it a few times – it'll take him a week to recover.

...the prostate

The only way to scratch this baby's backside is to stick a well-lubed finger up his bum (you may want to suit up in latex before you dive in).

5. Show off.

Form a snug fist around the base of his shaft (slathering on some lube makes this manoeuvre slicker and easier). Then glide your hand up his penis, gripping it firmly. Once you reach the top, twist your wrist and open your hand so the flattest part of your palm is resting on the head. Caress it – alternating back-and-forth and circular motions – for just a few moments. Then grip the shaft, with your palm around the head, and work downward with closed fingers. Repeating this wrist-twist trick while upping your speed will take him to the brink of an incredible climax (or push him over the precipice).

6. Show your muscles.

Many women don't have the first idea how to handle a penis. They grab, fumble, then give up. The amount of hands-on pressure that would make you say 'Ouch' will very likely make him say 'Ooooh, yeah'. Men's skin tends to be thicker, and their nerve endings aren't as close to the skin's surface as women's are. Use as much pressure as you would when shaking your boss's hand – hard enough to make an impression, but not so hard you leave a dent.

ONE ALL-TIME TECHNIQUE FOR YOU TO MASTER

The Quickie: when you understand that the average man thinks about sex about five billion times every day, you begin to see why he may want to launch his rocket in just 5 minutes or less.

YOUR IDEA OF FOREPLAY VS HIS

- Navel lingus and sucking other body parts **versus** you saying yes

- Sharing endearments in bed **versus** talking dirty in bed

- Full hands and mouth rub-down **versus** no hands blow-job

- Shaving his back **versus** him shaving your pubic hair into a bull's-eye shape

- Teasing at every stage of lovemaking – doing it bit by bit and so painstakingly that you're begging him to go all the way **versus** cutting to the chase

- Kissing your mouth **versus** kissing his penis

- Making love partially clothed **versus** being totally naked with the lights on, the window blinds up and lots of foot traffic outside

- Making love between once a day and once a week **versus** making love between once an hour and once a day

- Saying, 'I love you' **versus** saying, 'I want you'

GET BLOWN AWAY

Sex that sucks and blows at the same time

Perfect blowjob

1. Get **underneath** him as if you were making love in the missionary position (except that this time your mouth is where his love organs are).

2. Covering your **teeth with your mouth** so you look like you've had a bad session at the dentist, swallow him in one go. The trick is not to gobble him like a sausage, but to use a **hard sucking motion**. See how deep you can take him in without gagging (you need at least half of the shaft – unless he's huge and then a third is okay).

TIP Deep throating is a learned technique. Throw your head back as far as possible. This opens the throat and allows you to accept a long object. Lying on your back with your head over the edge of the bed is the most comfortable way to hold this position. Unless you have the lungs of Godzilla, you'll need to breathe – do it through your nose or around his penis on the outstroke.

3. Start **licking** to make it slick with spit. Then alternate rubbing with your hand and sucking.

4. Concentrate on the head, **rotating** it between your lips. A hard tongue along the underside will also make his toes curl.

5. Move on to **his balls**. Gently suck and scrape your teeth against them. If you can, take both of them in your mouth at once and gently suck, wiggling your tongue around.

6. Now get down to business. You'll need to master the art of **multitasking** and in this instance that means coordinating your lips, mouth, tongue and hands. First, put your thumb and index finger together, forming a tight ring at the base of his main man. Then wrap your lips around his penis and slide your mouth and hand up and down in unison. Or pinch your thumb and index finger together and squeeze them in an up-and-down motion on the ridge that runs along the underside. Then squeeze the sac under his balls between the same two fingers and use that up-and-down motion to manipulate his balls. It's dynamite: the motion is similar to milking and produces an intense orgasm that will leave him moaning (some say it's like having two orgasms in a row).

TIP Give him a hummer – put the first 5 cm (2 in) of his penis in your mouth and make a low, vibrating noise in the back of your throat. At the same time, use your hands on the bottom of his shaft and testicles for extra stimulation.

7. As he gets closer to **coming**, he'll set the pace. Just relax and go with it. If you want to opt out of swallowing, start licking his balls or the base of his penis, and keep on stroking his shaft as he's about to ejaculate.

PC TIP It's up to you whether you let him come in your mouth but it's best not to freak and spit if he does – although it feels like a lot, it's actually no more than a teaspoonful.

REAL TIP Don't believe him – he DOES want you to swallow. With love. Here's how: when he's about to come (he'll start pumping faster than a jackhammer), eliminate gagging by manoeuvring so that his shooting end points at your cheek instead of down your throat. (BUT, if you can't stand the stuff, you can now discreetly spit it into a pillow.)

Perfect **mouth sex** (tell him he will be tested later)

1. **He should not dive straight in.** Rather, he needs to treat your groin like some exotic animal he is trapping – move in slowly toward your inner thighs, then back away to the lower stomach region, move in, back away. Repeat several times until you are squirming.

TIP Make sure you are clean down there – most guys usually take this opportunity to give you the Sniff Test.

2. He should **warm things** up by spreading your vaginal lips and running his tongue up and down the entire area.

3. It's time to **slip his tongue inside** you, making it hard and stiff and using it like his penis. The purpose – to drive you out of your mind.

TIP He should never blow inside your vagina – it could cause infections.

4. Now you want some attention to your **love button**. If your clitoris hasn't popped up, he can bring his tongue to the top of your vaginal lips and gently suck and lick. As your clitoris rises to attention, he should gently pull the lips away and flick his tongue back and forth across it very quickly. He can follow this up by pressing his tongue hard against your clitoris. This should cause your legs to shudder.

5. As you start **zooming** towards orgasm, he can make his lips into an O and take the button into his mouth so he can suck.

TIP Push his head down and lift your pelvis up if you want him to suck harder. Some men act like a giant cat gently lapping at a saucer of milk. He needs to get his whole mouth down there and concentrate on gently rotating or flicking his tongue on your clitoris.

6. To heat things to **sizzling,** he can slip two fingers inside your vagina while adoring your love button. One is too skinny and three is too wide and therefore can't get deep enough. He should make sure they're wet so he doesn't irritate your skin. Keeping his mouth on your clitoris, he can slide his fingers inside, slowly at first, and then start moving them in and out rhythmically.

7. Two words for him: **don't stop**. Most men stop too soon. When your orgasm begins, he should hang onto your clitoris for the duration. When you start to come down from the first orgasm (yes, you read right), he can press his tongue along the underside of the clitoris.

TIP If he lightly continues the stimulation, you'll experience multiple orgasms.

INCENTIVE A woman stays excited for a full hour after she's had an orgasm. Make sure he realizes the full impact of that information. One woman is known to have clocked 56 orgasms. Does he know what effect he would have on a woman to whom he gave 56 orgasms? She'd be his for as long as he wanted her.

THE **SECRETS** OF GREAT ORAL SEX

For men and for women, it's mainly a matter of crossing your Ts.

TEASE Don't just dive in and stay there. Be a dip and dive oral lover.

TOUCH Whether it's fingers or tongue, keep it light.

TRACE Outline features such as his penile ridge with the tongue.

TONGUE Try lapping as you would an ice-cream, using longer strokes and a flat tongue.

TANTALIZE Create a steady rhythmic motion, and then stop for a moment before beginning again.

What scares his penis

Say or do the following and your boy will be one very limp hotdog.

Share flashbacks.
Rule of thumb: tell your man as much about past sexual exploits as you would tell your parents – like them, he'll assume you've had a few partners but he doesn't really want to think about it or hear all the gritty details.

Ask if you look fat (if you need to ask, you do).

Commit sexual perjury.
You could tell him he is the best lover you ever had, but then he may believe you and never improve.

Tell him all those cute little things that your pet does – in baby talk.
Coddling a pet makes a man suspect that your ideal companion is completely dependent on you for food, let's you dress him up in colourful wool jumpers and can be castrated if he starts acting too frisky.

Flirt with his brother, best friend, dad.
These are the people that he has to compete with on a daily basis, for heaven's sake.

Fear that, after having sex or upon seeing his penis for the first time, you'll ask, 'Is that all?'

He knows he's a normal size – after all, he's measured himself dozens of times, but do YOU know he's a normal size? How do you even know what's normal? What if your last lover was huge? And so on and so on.

Mention that your friend just got engaged.

All he'll hear is, 'I want to be engaged, buy me a ring, make me pregnant, sell your sportscar for an SUV.'

Tell him you have your period.

No matter how together they think they are, many men quake when confronted with a few drops of blood.

Tell him your period is late.

It would be less of a worry if you said, 'Honey, I think I accidentally called your boss a jerk earlier today' – his life of independence flashes before his eyes.

Carry around your really big vibrator.

All he can think is that you need that much to satisfy you and he does not have that much.

Try kissing him after going down on him.

Although men like to joke that they'd give themselves oral sex if they could, most freak over mouth-to-mouth contact after you've given them a blowjob because they're afraid of tasting anything that's just tasted them.

And be aware that when you have the **Home Bed Advantage**, he's scared he's going to discover one of the following: **1.** your stuffed-animal collection, **2.** too much hair stuff, or **3.** a jumbo pack of condoms.

When any guy sees a whole heap of make-believe characters in your home – animals/girl dolls/any useless stuff such as unicorns, trolls, etc. – he worries you are living in la-la land. He'd rather be with a woman who lives in the third planet from the sun. He doesn't really care if he sees medicine cabinets bulging with emollients, toners, lipsticks, mascaras – in fact, toothpaste, deodorant and Q-tips bode well in his mind for a budding romance, But an arsenal of weirdly shaped cylinders, bushy cones on sticks, clips with teeth and bendy foam snakes he reads as controlling – and if you are this controlling of your looks, what on earth would you do with humans? And sure, buying in bulk is good for household staples like cereal and toilet paper, but unless you want to cause a panic attack in the middle of some heavy action, **stash the condoms**.

How he can scare your vagina

What can turn you colder than an ice cube in the Antarctic.

Not warning you before he climaxes
Sperm tastes like sea water mixed with egg white.
Not everybody likes it.

Funky-tasting spunk (after all, it's not like it ever tastes that good)

If he falls asleep during sex
It's bad enough when he doesn't make sure you come –
when he doesn't bother coming to the party himself, it
can hurt a girl where she lives.

Pig Pecker Man (he needs to be a team player)

Amnesia Sex (your life has sunk to new depths)

When he asks for updates like 'did you come?'
He thinks he's being sensitive but he's really saying, 'Are you
done because I really want to catch the end of the game.'

Goalies
It may seem to him that humping for an hour without
climaxing is the mark of a sex god, but to you it's more
likely the mark of a numb vagina.

When he pushes your head down

He's worried you won't be able to find it – could this really be some primitive positioning system?

When he doesn't take his socks off

Does this mean that he thinks his feet are going to smell even worse than his socks?

When he insists on taking his pants off first

A man in socks and underpants is a man at his worst. He should always, but always, lose the socks first.

Flashbacks

Your head instantly fills with visions of a sexual acrobat, and you start to feel as desirable as a used condom. If the words 'stunning' and 'heartbroken' occur in the same sentence, feel free to knee him in the crotch.

When he asks what's your favourite fantasy

He does not really want to hear how you would like to sleep with his brother/both your best friends/your boss – all at the same time – while they tease your private parts with a feather/rubberband/pot of yogurt.

Three things you always want to hear

1. 'I can't wait to see you.'
2. 'I love waking up with you.'
3. 'I brought you something.'

HOW TO SHAKE HANDS WITH YOUR VAGINA

'I'm such a good lover because I practise a lot on my own.' The typical woman is prepared to burn the midnight oil learning how to master a man's body, but she forgets to figure out how to work her own equipment. When was the last time you two had a real heart-to-heart?

Men just have to look down to get acquainted with their best friend but women need a mirror, a light and a map. The first thing to is find yourself some Cliterature to put you **in the mood**. Then lie down and get comfortable. Find your clitoris and start playing with yourself. Most women prefer to use the index and/or middle finger. Just rub it aimlessly and pretty soon – possibly within seconds – you'll experience one full-fledged orgasm after another.

12 reasons to masturbate right now

1. Orgasm guaranteed.
2. To burn off energy.
3. To get revved up for a date.
4. It helps you figure out what you enjoy during sex.
5. At least you're having sex with someone you like.
6. You don't have to get dressed up first.
7. It has to be the ultimate safe sex – you can't get pregnant, and there's no chance of heartbreak or STIs/STDs.
8. You don't have to make your bed first.
9. You'll never hear, 'I hate condoms...'
10. You don't have to worry about taking too long.
11. You know you'll still be there in the morning.
12. Again, orgasm guaranteed.

M&Ms

You don't have to let the pleasure stop short with your own hand. Why do you think almost every porno flick has some babe wanking? Because men get off on it. Besides, M&M is the safest sex you can have with someone else – plus you are both **guaranteed** to get **what you want.** It's also a good move for when you have your period and he is not into sex or if he doesn't have the right touch so you have to take things into your own hands.

You can make the leap from solo to partner masturbation with minimum effort (and maximum orgasmic return). Just put your hand where you want and **let the games begin** – he might decide to work with you, attend to his own needs or sit back and watch. Polish yourself off and hopefully he'll get the hint that it's okay to do the same. Or tell him you like to watch (and then do – it's probably the best way to find out what really makes him yodel).

WELCOME TO **FANTASY** ISLAND

We all have fantasies that we'd never admit to our best friends, let alone our lovers. So what does it mean if you masturbate while thinking about how your overbearing boss criticized you? That you are probably going to have an orgasm.

Unless you feel like going through years of analysis, it probably isn't that important what you fantasize about as long as no one gets hurt. Now if you want to know what HE gets off on mentally, check out porn magazines. Men's fantasies tend to be more about lust and instant gratification. Just accept it as a fact of life.

A lot can go wrong if you share your fantasy with your lover. Some are physically impossible, legally impossible

or simply impossible (you can't get all the players together).
Or you may freak him out so much that he does a Date
Dump at some point. Or he may want quid pro quo action
on his fantasy (the one that involves you and your best
friend and lots of massage oil).

Which is why our sexual fantasies are generally best left
(separately) to the imagination.

Two for the price of one

Men tend to get off on lesbian sex, but women aren't
turned on by the male equivalent. The reason?

For men

It's double the pleasure. Men like watching the female-
female scenario for the obvious reason that there's no guy
poking around. Also, since men are highly visual, they can
imagine inserting themselves into the proceedings – and
they don't have to buy dinner for either woman.

For women

It's double the pain. Two men having sex isn't usually a
big turn-on. Two hairy backs, two flabby bellies, two goofy
faces? Women are less visual and more tactile in their
approach to lovemaking. Frankly, they'd rather watch
Animal Kingdom. Instead, women love to fantasize about
some nameless stranger (male or female) who instinctively
knows how to satisfy all their erotic urges. You know –
those that aren't necessarily satisfied in real-life sex.

CAN YOU **TEACH** AN OLD DOG **NEW** TRICKS?

Emergency sex techniques that are guaranteed to improve his technique without him even noticing

He kisses like a vacuum cleaner.

In his mind, kissing = foreplay. So smooching is a first step toward getting his hands on the goods downstairs. And when a person is in a rush, said person tends to get sloppy. Of course, what he doesn't realize is that for you, kissing is an indication of what's to follow. So if the kiss falls flat, those goods are taken off the shelf permanently. Sometimes, all he needs is a gentle nudge in the right direction. So show off your own lingual skills and give him the kind of mouth-to-mouth action that you want. Pause for a second, look in his eyes, touch his face and whisper, 'Like this.' He'll follow you anywhere.

He's goes from foreplay to intercourse too fast.

It makes you feel like he's paying by the hour and trying to get his money's worth by cutting out nonessentials. You can put on the brakes by getting on top and slipping his penis under your vagina. This way, it can't pop up and try for a lucky dip before you're ready. Or even try tying him up and then going at your pace.

He rubs you the wrong way.

Some men don't seem to understand that your clitoris is not just a mini penis. Slide your hand on top of his and guide him, all the while stoking his ego by telling him you love it when he touches you like that, that he has it exactly right. He'll never figure out you were directing all the action and, hopefully, next time he'll remember what he did to please you last time.

He's a Vagitarian.

You can overlook a certain lack of skills in a lover, but not this one. Like pizza, even bad oral sex is good though good oral sex is much better. Go down on him and then swivel until you are in 69 position.

He mouths off.

If you feel like screaming, 'That's my vagina down there – not the last ice-cream in the Sahara!' use your pelvis to bump him away from areas that don't do it for you and nudge him towards your hotter zones. Or get in on the action by literally pointing where you want him – for example, slip your hand over your mons with two fingers left open just enough for your clitoris to poke through. He will instinctively head for the opening you've left.

He doesn't get it.

Guys go by specific signs. If your nipples get hard because his hands were cold when he touched them, he thinks you like having your nipples squeezed. If your vagina gets wet during foreplay because you are ovulating and it always gets wet when you are ovulating, he thinks it is calling for his penis. If you moan because he accidentally gave you a leg cramp, he thinks he is the best lover ever. If he is misreading your body signals, start putting his hands where you want them and when. If he tries penetration too soon, push him on his back and climb on top so you are in control of boarding, instead of moaning, cry, 'Get off my leg, you dumb lug!'

He's only into Retro-Sex.

Missionary is fine once in a while but about as interesting as meat and two veg as a steady diet. Mix in some spicy sauce by pushing him back and climbing on top before he knows what's hit him. Then take over.

When is he beyond repair?

Is he a **Fixer-Upper**? Not if you check more than one of the following.

- No matter how much you tell him what works for you, he insists his way is the best way.

- He has BHI – he won't even hear you when you tell him what works best for you.

- He worships his mother – she has given him the false belief that everything he does is wonderful.

- He's into DIY – if it's broke, then only he knows how to fix it.

- He still wears the clothes that he wore ten years ago – clearly this is not a person who changes with the times.

ONE LAST FABULOUS SUM-IT-UP TIP There are three essentials to being great in bed: 1. enthusiasm, and lots of it – don't just lie there; moan, giggle, wriggle and beg for more. 2. Use lots of spit. 3. Don't bite his penis (nips, yes; teeth, never).

CHAPTER THREE MEN OR 'FUNNY HOW WOMEN DO NOT NEED TO BE TOLD "YOU HAVE A BEAUTIFUL PUSSY."'

What do you call that soft, **fleshy** thing attached to the end of a **penis?**
A man.

HERE WE TAKE A LONG HARD LOOK AT PENISES – AND HOW HE REALLY FEELS ABOUT HIS MOST PRIZED POSSESSION.

PENIS ENVY

'There are a lot of fish in the sea – you throw the short ones back and the big ones you mount.' You've heard the party line: it's not the size that matters, it's how he uses it. But even guys don't believe that. He knows big breasts don't really do anything but he craves them all the same. And that's the real reason why your average man:

- has measured his penis at least once;
- automatically thinks (and claims) he's at least 2.5 cm (1 in) bigger than he really is; and
- will deny it but has almost certainly checked out far more penises than you have (or ever will).

Sure, sure, it's difficult for him to **accurately assess** his penis size. The damn thing is always growing bigger and smaller, and his point of view can be misleading. If he's in a locker room with other men, theirs may look bigger because he's seeing them in profile. He looks down at his own.

Whatever, the reality is the only XXXS most women want in life is their dress size. On the other hand, anything larger than 7 5 cm (3 in) wide and 25.5 cm (10 in) long is likely to require a crowbar. Generally, anything between 15.25 cm (6 in) and 20.25 cm (8 in) will do nicely, thank you.

Why do **porn stars** look bigger? It's more baloney than beef. You know the camera makes everything look fatter? In effect the lens adds about 2.5 cm (1 in) of length. Porn stars also trim their pubic hair and **inflate** themselves with a vacuum **pump**, temporarily engorging the organ with blood. The reality is that any porn star's penis will be 30 per cent shorter than it's advertised (just like Tom Cruise).

30%

SHAKE HANDS WITH HIS PENIS

Your basic Size Queen (i.e. most men) is as familiar with his penis as he is with the back of his hand. Chances are that you, on the other hand, only really know his member in three stages: when it's about to become erect, when it is erect and when it's just losing its erection (hopefully just after ejaculation).

No matter how many penises you have met in your lifetime, you may not really know how the damned thing works. The penis isn't just a roll of flesh with a tube down the middle (aka the urethra) for squirting pee and semen. Here's how to understand his equipment from his point of view, starting at the tip.

The head

Otherwise known as the glans, this is the most sensitive part of his equipment – the 'nerve centre'. Its size differs from man to man. The head of an uncut (or uncircumcised) penis wears a hood, a thick piece of skin called the foreskin. This acts like a cosy blanket over the head most of the time.

TIP The tiny piece of V-shaped skin on the underside of the head is the frenulum. Unlike women, men have no love buttons, like the clitoris or G-spot, that require the right action to trigger orgasm. The frenulum is the closest they come.

The shaft

This is the workhorse and bulk of the penis. The urethra at its centre is surrounded by spongy tissue. Normally limp and not very exciting to bring to a party (think empty balloons), during arousal it fills with eight times as much blood, turning the penis from something that fits comfortably in his pocket to a large and unwieldy body appliance. Unlike most mammals, no bone is involved in this process – just pure carnal lust.

TIP The ridge on the underside contains many nerve endings.

The base

The root of the penis is deep inside the body, reaching back underneath the prostate gland toward the anus. This is the sensitive tissue that some men find great pleasure in having stimulated through either their scrotum or their perineum (the area between scrotum and anus). It is this 'hidden' part of the penis that allows some men, who show no penile shaft when their cock is soft, to become a grower.

TIP He uses his penis for peeing and climaxing. But don't worry that he may confuse you with a toilet. To keep from peeing and ejaculating at the same time, his body has a clever valve that closes off the neck of the bladder during ejaculation.

The testicles

Beneath the penis, attached to the groin, sits the scrotum' (aka 'the twins', 'balls' or 'stepchildren'). This is where the whole enchilada happens. The scrotum houses a 24-hour baby maker: the testicles. It needs to be kept cool so the little guys don't suffocate. That's why your average man feels compelled to crotch tweak and/or give the world a full-view crotch shot whenever he sits down – he's just cooling his boys.

TIP The reason men wince even when someone else gets kicked in the groin is because the testes are rich in nerve endings. Which makes them a pleasure zone for him during sex.

MORE IMPORTANT TIP

The testicles are a good gauge of how close he is to blowing. If they have shrunk significantly, he's about to explode.

IS HE A SHOWER OR A GROWER?

Some men have penises that look fairly large all the time and get only a little bigger when erect. Some men have **micro penises** that inflate to amazing proportions. And some men stay puny most of the time. Unfortunately, you can't tell what sort of goods he has until you try them on. The main thing to remember is that the erection is a great equalizer.

TIP What you really want to avoid is a shrinker. The following can shrivel a relaxed penis by 5 cm (2 in) or more: cold weather, skinny-dipping in cold water, piranhas.

How can you tell if he's a perfect fit?

Women vary in size, too. Some have long vaginas, and some short. So if even if he really *is* packing a humungous one, he may be missing your sexual mark. That raises two questions.

If you feel the **tip of his penis** bump into something at the maximum thrust point, then he probably hit your cervix (or the diaphragm covering your cervix) and he's long enough to hit the hot spots. If it feels like he's hitting so hard that you want to cry out (in pain, not pleasure), he's probably a little on the long side. And if you're not feeling anything at all, he is probably driving a mini.

And what can you do if he's not?

Men can do a few things to **upgrade their equipment**, ranging through surgery or injections of body fat to penis pumps, cock rings, exercise and herbal supplements (see page 100). But none of them solve your problem NOW. See pages 102–5 for emergency measures and lovemaking positions to suit you.

Equipment Failure

Speed Shooter

On most things – when to call after the first date, when to get together again, when to call it a relationship, when to book the caterers, when to think about nannies – a **woman's timing** is faster than a man's. But when it comes to orgasms, he leaves her in the dust. It becomes a problem when he is ejaculating faster than you can say, 'Is it in yet?' You could take his accelerated lovemaking as a supreme compliment – you are so amazing, he simply could not hold back. Or you could do something about it.

First, here's what will not slow him

- Psychoanalysis
- Getting drunk
- Using one or more condoms
- Concentrating on something other than sex while having sex, such as why his team is losing, his bank overdraft or the Irish potato famine
- Biting his cheek as a distraction
- Frequent masturbation
- Creams that numb the penis
- Testosterone injections
- Tranquillizers

...And here's what **might work**

Practise getting to the edge of orgasm, then stopping all penis-centred action and moving on to other body parts. It's tough but tantalize him with this bit of information – he longer he can hold off, the better he will become at **separating ejaculation and orgasm**, which means he could start having multiple orgasms.

Stop and squeeze.
This method is not highly recommended – basically, when you sense he is about to shoot, you stop what you are doing and grab the base of his penis to cut off sensation. There is nothing sensual about it and it often leaves him feeling like a gearstick.

Go ahead and let him come.
Then he can get on with the business of pleasing you without his pesky erection getting in the way. And who knows? He may even get hard again.

The Zen of sex fluids

His

Semen Some people think the food guys eat has an impact on sperm taste. Food containing naturally occurring sugars, such as fruit (and even real ale), is believed to produce a finer vintage. Red meat and diets rich in dairy produce may not go down so well, so guys should go easy on milk and cheese, as well as onions and garlic. Smoking, alcohol and coffee are also thought to mess with the taste, as will poor health and any medication.

- The average serving size of ejaculate is ½ to 1 tsp
- Main ingredients: protein, citric acid, fructose, sodium and chloride
- Nutritional content: 5 calories per tsp
- Protein content: 6 milligrams per tsp
- Reproductive material: 1 tsp of ejaculate can contain more than 600 million sperm. Sperm can live two to seven days in a woman's body.

Smegma This cheesy white stuff is nature's way of separating the foreskin from the head of the penis. It can build up on an uncircumcised penis, accumulating under the foreskin, but it is normal and harmless. The female equivalent has an equally alluring name; leucorrhoea.

Hers

White fluid when you climax
You are not peeing. It's the female equivalent of semen (without the sperm, of course). Think of it as proof that you just had one helluva orgasm. These juices are produced by the Skene's glands, located in a woman's urethra and made of tissue similar in composition to a man's prostate gland.

White sticky fluid and you didn't
This has the sexy name of leucorrhoea. It's secretions from the vaginal walls and your vagina's way of spring cleaning. It is slightly acidic to keep infections away.

TIP Ejaculate can stain clothes and upholstery (not something you want to explain to your parents). To remove, sponge with cold water. No good? Try diluted ammonia or vinegar. Last resort: try a remover for pet stains (it contains certain stain-busting enzymes).

Erection Meltdown
or 'Wait. I think it moved!'

Most things – vacuum cleaners, interns, your elbow – either work or they don't. But **erections** are a lot more complicated. A penis can apparently be in perfect working order and still refuse to stand and deliver. All men will experience dead pecker from time to time. This is guaranteed. When it happens, it is important for both you and him to realize that this may not be his fault – unless, of course, he is guilty of penis abuse and set fire to the poor thing or has been regularly whipping it. But even if a penis hasn't been literally misused in any way, there are still any number of reasons why equipment failure can happen.

There might be something on his mind.
Rather than make suggestions ('you're obviously worried about getting fired'), it might be better to ask him.

There might be something in his body that has caused his penis droop.
Certain antidepressants may wilt his penis while lifting his mood. And don't assume that a drug is safe just because it's sold over the counter. Antihistamines (found in cold and hayfever remedies), naproxen (found in some pain relievers), ibuprofen (also found in some pain relievers), and some sleeping pills can interfere with erections. So check labels and get him to talk to his doctor if you both suspect this could be the culprit.

Sometimes a condom can make him go numb.
Shop around for a thinner brand.

His penis doesn't like its position.

Some moves are better than others for maintaining erections. If he's on his back, it's possible he has a penis leak, that is the blood is actually flowing out of his penis rather than staying in and keeping him hard. Any position that causes his penis to bend in an unusual or painful way can also interfere with erections by replacing a pleasurable, erection-friendly sensation with a painful, erection-dampening one. For a while, until he gets his groove back, stick to the missionary position. If he's on top, gravity's helping blood to pool in his penis.

He could be really tired.

He could be really drunk.

He could be playing with himself too much.

There's nothing wrong with a practice session now and then. But athletes who overtrain can end up losing the race. The danger: he becomes so accustomed to getting it exactly the way he likes it that any woman who tries to please him is bound to fail.

His penis is tired.

It needs as much shut-eye as it can get. Every night while he sleeps, he has three to five hour-long erections. You probably noticed this phenomenon the last time he had to pee at 4 am. Those erections are not there to make life interesting for you. They work to recharge his penis – by keeping it nourished with oxygenated blood. Theoretically, the more nocturnal erections he has, the more flexible his erectile tissue will become.

He could be smoking too much.

Smoking is a known cause of impotence. And there's some evidence that smoking can affect erection size too because it damages blood vessels and also penile tissue itself, making it less elastic and therefore preventing it from stretching during arousal.

He could be cheating.

Often, if a guy is getting some action on the side, he feels guilty when he's with the one he's been cheating on and the guilt literally kills his erection.

He could be really scared of his penis.

If things didn't go well the last time he tried sex, this time is going to be even more difficult because he is replaying the last time over and over in his head.

He could be really scared of you.

He thinks you're a 15 on a scale of 1 to 10, that you'll discover he's full of before-play, that you'll discover you have been dating down. To re-inflate, you must act like you worship his penis and its owner until their egos are both back to full size again.

He helped a friend move and now he has convinced himself that he has a hernia.

He saw someone bigger than him and now he's embarrassed.

In the case of erection meltdown,

remember that a watched kettle never boils, and a watched penis never hardens. **Let him hold you** instead of you sympathetically holding him. It'll make him feel more manly – and ergo, perhaps – more horny.

- Do not say, 'Does this always happen?' or 'I didn't feel like it anyway.' Comments like this have the same effect as throwing a bucket of cold water on his penis.
- Don't grab it and try to solve the problem by shaking or squeezing. It'll just make him even more self conscious.
- Do not use the word 'impotence'.

Two more **things to do instead**

1. Just **concentrate on you** – have him use this time to
get on better terms with your equipment. It might take
the pressure off his penis and trick it into working again.

2. If, after 15 minutes, he's still deader than a dodo down
there, put it away for another day.

Are you on the same cycle?

While some men are virtual sexual camels, others
tend to feel backed up if they go a day without.

To figure out his **cycle:** try avoiding sex until he
gets downright pissed off. If it happens after two
weeks, then you know he needs sex at least once
every 14 days (it's up to you what you decide to
do with this information).

To find his **high end:** just start initiating sex
until he refuses. Now you know how much
loving he can take in one cycle.

If the amount of sex you need to be satisfied falls
within his range, then the two of you are sexually
compatible. But if he wants more or less than
you, someone is going to end up unsatisfied.

BUILDING A BETTER PENIS

Men can do a few things to upgrade their equipment:

- SURGERY This is the only way to get a bigger boat, permanently. The ligaments that attach the penis to the pubic bone are snipped so the penis hangs lower and looks larger. But it's expensive, he loses his ability to aim straight, it makes his erection wobbly (with a greater risk of fracture) and it doesn't make sex any better.

- SHOTS Body fat can be injected under the skin of the shaft to make it thicker. And lumpier, since the injections end up clumping.

- PENIS PUMPS If his erections tend to be less than fully inflated, a pump-induced stiffy might be a tad more impressive because the contraption forces blood in to the penile area. But afterward it can be harder to ejaculate. Plus, pumps can cause bruising. And once the erection's gone, the penis is unchanged,

- COCK RINGS These do make him look and feel bigger by trapping blood in the penis. So he can stay stiff longer. (See also page 300.)

- EXERCISE AND WEIGHTS There aren't any muscles in the penis to beef up. But strengthening those he has can give him stronger erections and orgasms and more control over when he lets go.

- HERBAL AND CHEMICAL SUPPLEMENTS The effects of herbal supplements are minuscule but ginkgo biloba and ginseng are said to help. Viagra, on the other hand, can have huge effects but not for everyone, it can also cause urinary tract infections and headaches.

CARE AND FEEDING
OF PENISES

People don't name their hands or their shins. Women do not name their private parts (have you ever heard a woman address her vulva as 'Lil' Amy' or refer to 'Big Virginia the Vagina'?). But men choose to identify their penises in a manner that suggests that their gear has a life of its own, like they are a couple of buddies that get together once in a while to live it up.

They also somehow believe that naming their dicks absolves them of responsibility for their actions. Impotence, premature ejaculation, unsafe sex or plain bad taste in partner choice all become the work of Big Al instead of just Al. Perhaps if guys insist on naming their penises and treating them like separate individuals with wills of their own, they should be required to carry a permit to have one. Just like a pet. Then, if his dick breaks out and starts making any kind of unwelcome problem, the police should have the right to arrest it and make him pay a whacking fine to get it back again.

The top ten names and what they mean

Dipstick He practices the Withdrawal Method.

John Thomas He's married and gave you a false name just in case you turn out to be a Bunny Boiler.

Love muscle It's the only muscle on his body.

Little (his name) or Junior It's the only child he'll ever want.

Big (his name) That's the one who makes all the decisions.

Captain Fantastic He wishes.

Wee-Wee He calls his mother every day.

Dick He has a singular lack of imagination.

Tool Don't expect him to have any mastery over it.

Mr Stiffy Expect impotence or speed-shooting problems.

How to make the most of the tool he has

Having sex is no great achievement. Insert Tab A into Slot B, and it's done. Good sex, however, is a little more complicated and a hell of a lot more fun. To achieve that, you first have to take a look at what he's bringing to the party. Really, take a look at it. Is it long? Short? Wide? Knotted? Here's the different types of penises and how to make the most of what he's got.

Short Pecker – erect length under 11.5 cm (4½ in)

If his penis is so minuscule that you have trouble distinguishing it from, say, a probing finger, he had better be really amazing with his mouth and digits or you are going to feel like you've just had your annual gyno check-up. If he's not quite that small but still on the puny size, have him ride high, bringing the base of his penis up against your clitoris. Then, instead of thrusting, he can rub and grind against your pubic bone. Since he's not thrusting, it doesn't matter how long or short he is; it's all in the rocking motion.

TIP Try trimming his pubic hair. A careful cut snipped 1 cm (½in) or so around the base of his penis will make him look 4 cm (1½ in) longer. Don't do this after drinking.

Thin Pecker / erect girth 13.5 cm (5¼ in) or less

For men with narrow penises, it's all about friction. Women don't usually have a problem with thin guys, but some men say they can't achieve enough sensation and they feel like they're lost inside the vagina. If this has often been his experience, the best lovemaking position is one in which your knees are together and your vagina is stretched from front to back, not side to side. You can either lie flat on the bed or tuck your legs up against your chest. This will pull your vaginal lips together, tightening your grip on his erection and creating a lot of extra friction.

TIP A great position for a man with a long, thin penis is to enter from behind while you lie flat on your stomach. This reduces depth and increases tightness.

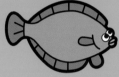

Lard Pecker / erect girth over 13.5 cm (5¼ in)

This is one case where fat is good. What most guys don't realize is that how wide he is counts more than how long he is. Still, what you don't want is a tight fit or you could end up feeling like you have carpet burns on your vagina.

TIP The more aroused you are, the more your vagina will expand. So simply waiting for you to get wet isn't good enough. He has to wait several minutes more, until you're fully engorged. Then use a little saliva or lube to moisten his penis before entry. Back him in via your rear for maximum pleasure.

Long Pecker / erect length 16.5 cm (6½ in) or more

He'll never believe you, but an extra long penis is questionably desirable since it's apt to penetrate too deeply and pain the delicate cervix. When you're in the mood for love, the last thing you want is a faux smear test. Here the missionary position works best because that's where you tend to get the least depth of penetration.

TIP With length comes responsibility. He shouldn't thrust too deeply when he's on top. Or else he can lie back and let you straddle him with your knees. Then, when you want to use the top of his penis, you can keep your knees close to his body and thrust gently against the tip of his erection. If you want more, you can slide your knees outward and lower yourself just as far as is comfortable.

Average Pecker / erect length 11.5–16.25 cm 4¹/₂–6¹/₄ in)

Most of the vagina's nerves are located in its outermost third, the area this one is best equipped to delight. Think about it: what's better – a run-of-the-mill pecker whose size is just perfect for targeting all the most sensitive spots in your vagina or the guy who uses his full length to drill for gold?

TIP An average-sized man can better target this sensitive outer third of your vagina by entering from on top while you lie with your legs flat. This reduces the depth of penetration by preventing your pelvises from coming together completely. (It is also a good position for oversized guys.) In addition, when your legs are extended, the position puts more tension on your vaginal lips, and this improves the stimulation for both of you.

Curly Pecker / erect angle 90 degrees or more

The more directly skyward his penis points, the less flexible his erection is and the more careful you have to be when using it, especially when gyrating on top. Also, deep upward thrusts can put uncomfortable pressure on the back wall of your bladder, which can give you the urge to pee mid-action. On the plus side, he possesses the perfect penis to rub your G-spot. Use the missionary position, but keep his pelvis low and make shallow thrusts. Steep, stubby men are doubly blessed. They can keep the head of the penis within that first sensitive section of the vagina and stimulate the G-spot at the same time.

TIP If his angle is steep, try sitting up against the headboard during lovemaking to improve the alignment.

Cut Pecker

Circumcised guys have one major advantage – less chance that you may have to shout mid-meal, 'Hold the mayo' about his smegma. But still, those clean uncircumcised penises do hold some advantages: handjobs are less likely to require lube (more skin = less Indian burns); a foreskin may provide extra friction for the woman during extended intercourse; and the head is probably more sensitive during arousal, as it wears a protective coat the rest of the time. However, for the most part, a foreskin makes very little difference – when erect, the cut and the uncut are almost identical.

Pig Pecker

He'll say he can't help it. So you say *you* can't help it when you accidentally give his porker a little nip during some mouth action.

Bi-Polar Pecker

If he's up, down and everywhere in between, cut your losses – a man can get an erection when the door closes and the draught hits his crotch. (This is one reason men suffer from BHI – one minute he is listening closely to your latest business strategy and the next, all he can think about is how to stand up without Mr Stiffy pitching a tent right into his Caesar salad.) But if it's just an occasional droop, grab a hair scrunchie that's not too tight. After he's fully erect, wrap it around the base of his testicles and the base of his penis (twice if it's too loose). It should be tight without cutting off circulation. Then he'll fly at full mast until you're ready for him.

Dribbling Pecker

He drools instead of shoots when he climaxes. Strengthening the muscle that lies around the base of the penis can increase the strength of ejaculation and the intensity of orgasm. Called the pubococcygeus muscle, it also surrounds the prostate and anus, and he can tone up by squeezing the muscle he uses to control his pee flow. This exercise can be done any time, although it is more pleasurable when he has an erection, since it increases blood flow in the penis and the pressure on sensitive areas at its tip.

Dead Pecker

Give him two headache pills and call him in the morning.

The five **worst things** you can do to his penis

1. Forcing down what's gone up

Downward pressure on an erect penis strains the suspensory ligaments, the two tendons that attach the penis to the pubic bone and prop it up when erect. If stretched too far, they lose their ability to hoist his member so that his erections point out or down, not up.

2. Forcing sex before it's ready

His penis does not respond well to premature attempts at intercourse and can sustain bending and buckling injuries which damage the structures that fill with blood when he gets an erection. The result? A penis that permanently bends, sometimes painfully, in one direction or another.

3. Poor zipper management

You sexily and seductively pull down his zipper for a little hanky panky and then ouch! Here's what to do. Rub oil around the zipper (it lubricates things). Then try pulling the zipper back in one swift motion. Don't fiddle; you'll end up making matters much worse. Assess the damage and, if necessary, apply antiseptic cream and a bandage to stop the bleeding. Bad as they look, zipper injuries rarely cause lasting harm, but they are very painful. If you can't unhook him, take him off to Emergency where they'll cut the zipper apart with metal clippers under anaesthetic.

4. Using a stand-in lubricant

If you discover that the tube is flat, do not raid your hair, kitchen or first-aid supplies for an alternative. Don't use anything on his genitals (or yours) unless it has been approved by several doctors for application in that area. You risk putting put holes in your latex protection, causing allergic reactions and even chemical burns.

5. Using it as a vaulting pole

Penile fracture can be caused if his penis is rammed against your pelvic bone. So when on top, don't lift up more than 2.5–5 cm (1–2 in) on the upstroke. And never lean back against his erection while he's inserted. Also it's usually better to withdraw when changing positions. If he does fracture, you'll know. His penis will turn purple and swell up. Don't dawdle: go quickly to Emergency. He will need surgery.

THE SEVEN STAGES OF MAN

What he feels, thinks, wonders and wants when he's making love to you.

Stage1: Getting in the mood

What puts a man in the mood for sex? Your naked body. Failing that, a glimpse of your cleavage, telling him you aren't wearing knickers, stretching in a way that shows bare skin – anything that makes him THINK of your naked body.

Stage 2: Initial arousal

Once he has an erection, all he wants is to fuck you and all he can think about is how to accomplish this. But, because he knows there are rules, he will go through the motions and kiss you.

Stage 3: Serious foreplay

All the foreplay he needs is driving back to your place. But because he knows you need more, he will work his way down your body crossing things off like it's a To Do list. Lips? Got them. Breasts. Check. Clitoral action? Fine? This is not to say he is not enjoying himself – but he prefers to proceed in an orderly fashion.

Stage 4: The plunge

What he's been waiting for. Aaaah, bliss.

Stage 5: The verge

All is going according to plan. He's near orgasm – he thinks you may be too, but all he can concentrate on is himself.

Stage 6: The climax

Here he comes. The several seconds during which a man releases are often accompanied by a release of emotion – 'I love you' may slip out. He is not saying it to you, he is saying it to his penis (or, if he *is* saying it to you, he means 'I love you for having sex with me').

Stage 7: The afterglow

His post-orgasm mood depends on how he feels about you:
'Is this heaven?' (he's in love with you)
'I really need to get going so I can pay that bill' / 'I wonder how soon I can leave without her freaking out?' (he's just interested in you for sex)
'I really should compose a symphony/run a marathon' (sex with you makes him feel he can accomplish anything).

What he says/what his penis means

Men are like appliances – you need detailed instructions
to help you figure them out.

At the end of a first date, a man will generally use one of
these three basic lines:

1. **'I'll call you.'** You'll never hear from him again.
2. **'I had a really nice time.'** He'll call you next week
   if nothing more interesting is happening.
3. **'What are you doing tomorrow?'** He wants to
   know if he can stay over tonight.

'We're seeing each other.' It's down to you and one other woman.

He calls you 'girlfriend'. You've made him
breakfast, he fixed your car and his friends are not allowed
to come on to you.

'I only had a few beers.' I had more than one and less than 50.

'I really like you.' I think I am falling in love but if I
say that word there is no going back.

'I need some space.' I'm about this close to dumping but I haven't quite
worked up the nerve to do it yet.

'I'd love to take you to Bermuda.' I really
want to have sex with you.

'She's just a friend.' She is/was/hopefully one day soon will be my girlfriend.

'My ex won't stop calling me.' I'm not over my ex.

'It was a mutual thing' (talking about why his last relationship ended). She dumped his sorry butt.

'We haven't spoken in forever and I've been thinking about you.' I haven't gotten laid in almost three months.

'Let's just be friends.' I don't want you but could you to set me up with your hot friend?

'This is our third date isn't it? / Is it warm out or just me? / You think it's true what they say about oysters?' I WANT SEX

'You're incredible' (said straight after sex). Are you thinking about your ex and how much better he was than me?

'You're incredible' (said any other time). You're incredible.

ONE LAST FABULOUS SUM-IT-UP TIP

Men are just women with a couple of balls and a stick. Translation: You've got a whole body there not just six to eight inches of rigid flesh. Get to know your man-toy from head to toe – the more you use him, the more he'll want to use you.

CHAPTER FOUR SOCIAL INTERCOURSE OR 'THE BEST WAY TO GET OVER A MAN IS TO GET UNDER ONE.'

Women need a **reason** to have sex and **men** just need a **place.**

HERE ARE SOME EASY-TO-MASTER SEX MOVES TO EXPAND YOUR MATTRESS REPERTOIRE AND GET YOUR WORKOUT IN BED RATHER THAN AT THE GYM.

PUMP IT UP

Forget about the gym. You can buff a set of killer love muscles that'll give you bigger, more intense and just plain **more orgasms** without leaving home.

Find it and flex it

1. Sit on the **toilet** with your legs spread and pee.
2. Now try to **stop peeing** without moving your legs. Those are your pubococcygeus (PC, or pelvic floor) muscles.
3. **Squeeze them**, holding for 5 seconds, and then release. Now you know how to do the exercise that's also called 'Kegels'.

Once you know the what and the how, you can do the exercise anywhere: while driving a car, watching TV or during one of those boring work meetings (at least you will be using your time constructively). Work up to 15 repetitions, twice a day, and in two weeks you'll be in excellent sex shape.

Bring it on

- When he's **thrusting** in and out, squeeze really tightly each time before he re-enters, creating fabulous friction.
- Squeeze when you know he's **about to come**.
- Sit **on top** of him and when he's inside you, without thrusting, squeeze powerfully ten times.
- Do it **from behind** – once he's inside, begin contracting your muscles. You'll press his penis against the front wall of your vagina, where your G-spot lives.
- When he's inside, push out, then squeeze, and pull him part of the way back. **Push out, constrict, pull in** a little, and push out and constrict again until he explodes.

THIRTY GREAT SEX POSITIONS

Fashion or sex – there is no such thing as one-size-fits-all. But whether it's a slender member or below-the-belt parts that don't pair up, you can still be a perfect sexual fit. Here's a move for every moment and mood.

He's a Speed Shooter.

HOW IT'S DONE Slow him down to your time. Climb on top so that you can control how far he goes in and how long he stays there. If you think he's about to come, simply remove and scoot up his body so he can give you a thorough tongue whipping until you catch up.

You're in a Retro-Sex mood.

HOW IT'S DONE Three simple variations to up the orgasmic odds. Missionary does not have to mean Lottery Sex.

- He raises his body, resting his weight on his elbows or his outstretched arms. This puts greater pressure on your clitoris.
- He puts his legs outside yours while you keep yours close together. This will give you lots of friction as he enters.
- Raise your legs so that your knees are pressed to your chest and your legs are draped over his shoulders. This will make your vagina longer, letting him in more deeply and give you more friction and pressure where you crave it most.

Your mind is wandering. It's missionary time again and instead of being in the moment, you start thinking about when the sales start or your upcoming bunion surgery or...

HOW IT'S DONE Get focused by switching to a position that lets you feel more of him inside you. Lie face-down on the bed with your pelvis slightly raised. It'll be more comfortable if you add a pillow for support. He enters from behind.

You want to pull an all-nighter.

HOW IT'S DONE Create a holding pattern by slipping side-by-side, face-to-face when you're on the brink. There's not a lot of movement and it'll bring you down a notch so you can crank things up again to an even hotter level.

You're in a rush.

HOW IT'S DONE If you're so horny you just want to get to the orgasm already, position yourself underneath him and clench your bottom and PC muscles at the same time. You'll lift your pelvis a little off the bed and increase blood flow to your pelvic area to make orgasm easier and more explosive.

You're in a rush and you're both clumsy.

HOW IT'S DONE Put your hands on a chair, desk, couch or wall, and lean forward with your butt in the air. Tilt your pelvis so he can slip inside. He should hold onto your hips to help steady himself as he thrusts.

You want the kind of orgasm that makes you think you're in love.

HOW IT'S DONE Graze all your hot spots in one fell swoop. Lie on the floor face-up, a couple of pillows propping your bottom. Keep your knees half-bent, your legs wide, and your arms high over your head. He enters you at a higher angle than usual, planting his hands on the floor beside your head and moves his penis in a circular motion while you move your pelvis in circles in the opposite direction.

8 You want him to work the directionals on your clitoris and he's much more interested in driving his penis into your vagi-port .

HOW IT'S DONE Stop his pounding by slipping into a position where you are both sitting while facing each other. Then hold hands and lean back. This will limit his movement and force him to grind against your clitoris as he wriggles.

9 It's the morning after the night before.

HOW IT'S DONE Blood to the head will ease that pounding – as will a brain-melting orgasm (studies show that an orgasm is the best cure for a headache). He lies on his back, legs wide apart. Face his feet, straddle his hips on your knees and lower yourself onto his penis. Slowly extend your legs back toward his shoulders and relax your body onto the bed or ground between his feet. Your two pairs of legs should now form an X shape. Use your PC muscles and wriggle your bum.

10 He drives a mini.

HOW IT'S DONE Turn his compact into a Cadillac by lying flat on your back with your legs tucked up against your chest. Scrunching up this way will shorten your vagina and create a tight squeeze.

11 You're in a dominatrix mood.

HOW IT'S DONE Feel your power by having him lie on his back and lift his knees toward his chest. Facing him, squat down and straddle his legs so your thighs are hugging his. Lower yourself onto his penis – the closer he draws his knees to his chest, the better access you'll have to his main accessory. Bend your knees and move yourself up and down.

You're like a virgin to each other.

HOW IT'S DONE Take those making-love-with-each-other-for-the-first-time nerves off the boil by putting him on top. This will be the most comfortable position and require the least amount of effort from you (you have enough to think about). A pillow under your hips will also ease things along (besides making your body appear longer and sexier). AND, if you push your pelvis down as he enters you, it will to help relax things down there.

It's that time of the month.

HOW IT'S DONE Remove your tampon (a diaphragm or menstrual shield will plug things up temporarily, if needed). Both lie on your sides with him behind so he is looking at your back and tuck your bottom into his pelvis. Lift your top leg while he shifts his lower body into a half-kneeling position, entering you from behind. This useful half doggy-style, half spooning hybrid combines the cosy intimacy of lying side-by-side with G-spot-rubbing rear entry without ever making an issue of your period bloat.

PDA Sex

HOW IT'S DONE Five moves for when you want to stay fully clothed.

- On a chair (er, did you check that it's up to the job?): sit on his lap, undo his fly, pull your panties to one side and jiggle your hips.
- Lean on something (like a bathroom sink) and have him enter from behind.
- Wrap yourself around him as he holds you up (in an alley or walk-in wardrobe).
- In the car: face him with your knees up against your chest and your feet on the seat or hooked over the neck rest (use the seatbelts for added kinkiness).
- On the stairs: kneel in front of your partner one step up or, preferably, at the landing, both of you facing up. He enters you from behind. Because his penis has an upward tilt, he'll naturally hit your G-spot.

You have a humungous zit on your face.

HOW IT'S DONE Shift the focus with a rear-facing move. Lean over a table or any counter-top and wriggle your bottom. He'll be so transfixed by the view he won't care whether you have a face or not, let alone whether Mount Vesuvius is growing on it. If you really want to send him into blind oblivion, reach back and give his penis a loving squeeze mid-action.

You're going to fulfil his fantasy – what a babe!

HOW IT'S DONE Give him a lap dance. Get him to lie prone while you straddle him with your knees bent and your feet flat on the floor. While lifting your hips up and down, start rotating your pelvis so that you are grinding and pushing against him. He'll collapse in a quivering heap.

Staying connected when your heights don't match up.

HOW IT'S DONE IF HE'S HEAD AND SHOULDERS ABOVE YOU Sit on top of him – this way you can look into his eyes instead of counting his chest hairs.

HOW IT'S DONE IF YOU'RE TALLER THAN HI, EVEN IN FLATS Lie on top of him. You may be worried that he'll suffocate between your breasts, but he'll love the fact that his head is buried in your chest. The key to this one is not to make it obvious that you're compensating unless you want to see his erection melt faster than an ice-cream during a heat wave.

Lard sex

HOW IT'S DONE WHEN YOU'RE HAVING A FAT DAY Have him sit on the bed with his legs slightly apart and extended out in front of him. Straddle his lap on your knees and slowly lower yourself onto his erect penis. Lean back as far as you can, resting the top of your head on the bed, if possible. Reach back with your hands until you can grasp his feet. Your tummy will look amazingly thin.

HOW IT'S DONE IF HE HAS A BEER BELLY

A side move will let you work around his bulge. Lie on your back with your man to your right. He lies on his left-hand side. Bend and lift your right leg up. Your man arranges his right leg over your left and inserts his penis. This position ensures a nice leisurely pace. Crank up the pleasure factor by grinding your bottom tantalizingly against his pelvis.

He's an oversize.

HOW IT'S DONE Tell him to wipe that smirk off his face. To avoid feeling pricked, poked and pierced, lie on your back and close your legs. This will let you control how deeply he penetrates you while making sure his pet anaconda still gets fully massaged.

You need to add some sizzle – fast!

HOW IT'S DONE Give a twist to you getting on top. Have him lie on his back, with his legs spread slightly, his head propped on a pillow. Swing your legs over his body, keeping them together and at right angles. Sit on his thighs or in his lap, then lean back on your arms for support. Open your legs slightly as he enters you, and make slow, corkscrew motions.

He's clueless.

HOW IT'S DONE If he thinks that all he needs to do to get you off is act like a petrol tank (pump and fill), take things into your own hands by climbing on top. Then alternate between moving your hips in a steady circular motion and rocking them back and forth. This way, you'll feel him rub against each side of your vagina, and his pubic bone – the hard surface just above the shaft of his penis – will push your hot button.

You want the gold in synchronized orgasms.
HOW IT'S DONE Raise your right leg until your knee is level with his left shoulder. Your left leg stays flat on the bed. He then directs his thrusts toward the inner thigh of your raised leg. By splitting your legs, you stretch your vagina, allowing for tighter penetration and more pressure exactly where you crave it – on your clitoris.

He's got a thin dick.
HOW IT'S DONE If he feels more like a tickle than a torpedo, rev things up by lying down at the edge of a bed, desk or counter-top. Extend your legs straight upward, keeping them close together. You can put your hands under your bottom to lift your pelvis, use them to hold on to the bed or desk for leverage, or keep them free, as you prefer. He then enters you while standing up (or if the bed or desk is low, kneeling on the floor). He can grip your feet for leverage, which will give him the extra stability he needs to thrust more deeply. Keeping your legs together is guaranteed to make him feel fuller inside you.

He's ugly, but you're horny.
HOW IT'S DONE Slip into a position where you don't have to look at him but his penis is certain to locate your G-spot like a heat-seeking missile. Get down on all fours, as if crawling, and let him enter you from behind, either as he's standing or kneeling. Then, instead of staying on your hands and knees, lie flat on your stomach but tilt your bottom upward by placing a pillow under your pelvis. Now you're free to fantasize he's Brad Pitt (but just be sure to call out the right guy's name!).

You want more but he's limper than a lettuce leaf.

HOW IT'S DONE As long as he is at least as tall as you, you can have sex kneeling even if he isn't fully erect (as long as you don't try to stuff him inside you like a sausage). He sits on his raised heels and you squat over him, face to face, with your thighs spread, and guide his penis inside you. Once he's in, you can help take some of the weight off his back by leaning backward on one arm while holding on to him with the other hand.

You want to mew like a kitten.

HOW IT'S DONE To hit your clitoris every time, try what is very unsexily known as coital alignment technique (CAT). Instead of entering you straight when using the missionary position, he rides high so that his pubic bone is applying pressure directly to the rounded bit above your vagina where the clitoris hides. By settling into a gentle rhythm in which he rocks his pubic bone back and forth over your clitoris rather than focusing so much on thrusting in and out, you get stimulated in all the right places.

You're scared you might blurt the 'L' word mid-act.

HOW IT'S DONE Lock your lips by lying face-up and bringing your knees up to your chin. He enters you as he would in the missionary position while you rest your lower legs on his shoulders. Hold his upper arms for leverage while he grips your hips and, as he begins thrusting, lick, suck or nibble on his mouth.

He's a Ball Buster.

HOW IT'S DONE Avoid getting knocked out or even coming in to scary eye contact with those mutant globes by having him come at you from behind.

You're squeezing into a single bed.

HOW IT'S DONE Begin by lying on your back and then, with your legs and arms wrapped round him, gently roll over to one side. If there's too much weight on your lower leg, you can carefully slip both legs between his.

You're having three-ply sex.

HOW IT'S DONE WITH AN EXTRA MAN Have Man 1 lie on his back. Climb on top, facing him. Once he is inside you, have Man 2 work from behind, where he can rub himself against both of you while using his hands and mouth or, if you are big enough, try to work his way inside your vagina. If you are practising safe sex, he can also dive into your bottom from this position as long as you use plenty of water-based lubricant to keep the proceedings moving smoothly.

HOW IT'S DONE WITH AN EXTRA WOMAN One of the women lies flat on her back. The other climbs on top with her head by the first woman's toes and her feet by her head. Both women can then comfortably start a little mouth action on each other. The man can kneel between the legs of the woman who is lying on her back and the woman on top can help slip him inside and then continue with her tongue bath.

For you, any position where he reaches your love button or rubs his pubic bone against yours will rock your body. **For him,** it's any position that slows pressure on the penis, especially the tip (his personal hot spot). Positions that cover most of these bases are: you on top facing his feet, kneeling between his legs or rear entry with you bending between his legs. As a big bonus for you both: don't forget to squeeze your love muscles to caress the head of his penis as he thrusts toward orgasm.

UPDATE YOUR LOOK

Even sexual positions need to move with the times. Here are some simple ways to take a standard old move and make it modern.

The missionary

BASIC Typically you're on your back with your knees bent, while he's on top, supporting his weight with his arms.

ACCESSORIZED

- Wrap your legs around his waist or his neck.
- Have him hold your legs with his forearms under your knees.
- Put your legs on his shoulders. Some women say this increases G-spot stimulation.
- Pull your knees right up to your chest and then place both your feet flat against his chest.
- Pile pillows under your back or buttocks to change the angle and depth of penetration.

You on top

BASIC Like the name says, you sit or squat on top of him.

ACCESSORIZED

- Assume a riding position and lean forward, putting your weight on your hands.
- Stimulate your G-spot and clitoris by moving from side to side in small circles.
- Up the love-button friction by flattening yourself out on top of him, clenching your thighs together, and rolling your clitoris into him.

Rear entry

BASIC You're on all fours with him kneeling behind.

ACCESSORIZED

- Lower your chest to the bed, a move that elongates and tightens your vagina.
- Move to the edge of the bed so that he is standing behind you rather than kneeling. This gives him better control.
- Both lie on your sides, him facing your back, with one of his legs between yours.
- Lie half on your side, half on your back, bending the leg you're lying on.

SPIRITUAL QUICKIES

Forget about tantric celibacy, breathing through alternate nostrils and all those other new-age fads that are supposed to achieve nirvana. Face it, what you really want are new ways to stick his yang in your yin.

The Turtle

Position yourself so you and your man are sitting face to face, very close together, with his erect penis inside you. Then each link your elbows under your partner's knees and lift them up to chest level. In this position you can rock backward and forward, and the motion will have you chanting mantras.

The Wheelbarrow

Kneel on the floor with your arms crossed in front of you (cushioned by a pillow) and your behind in the air. Rest your head on your crossed arms (or brace your head on the floor itself if you find that more comfortable). Have your partner stand behind you and lift your legs up, holding your ankles, until your lower body is almost at right angles to the floor. Then he should enter your vagina from the rear. The deep impact will make you go head over heels.

The Backbend

Have your lover sit on the bed with his legs extended out in front of him. Straddle his lap on your knees and lower yourself onto his erect penis. Then lean into a back bend. (Be careful not to strain your lower back or his penis – if it hurts either of you, stop immediately) Rest the top of your head on the bed and reach back with your hands to grasp his feet. Most men think a knee bend is an Olympic feat, so he'll worship you as a sex goddess.

The Vine

Start with your lover sitting on a chair. Facing him, lower yourself onto his erect penis until you're sitting on his lap. Wrap your arms and legs tightly around him. Then have him cradle your lower back and buttocks while he slowly stands up. If he's been hitting the protein powder, he may even be strong enough to lift you up and down on his penis. Otherwise, he can make things easier on himself by propping your back against a wall for support or resting your rear on a table. Enjoy the ride (also a good move for water nymphs).

The Sweet Love

Lie on your back and pull your knees up to your chest. Your partner clasps your feet in his hands and thrusts from a kneeling position. The deep impact will nudge your G-spot. Variations: for more control, he can grasp your hips; for more pleasure, he can massage your clitoris.

The Pair of Thongs

Have your partner lean back against a stack of pillows with his legs hanging over the side of the bed. Then kneel astride his hips and lower yourself onto his erect penis. Brace your hands on the pillows behind your partner's head for added leverage and support. He can reach around and play with whatever sticks out.

The Upward Dog

Your partner lies flat on his back; you straddle him and lower yourself onto his erect penis. Then slowly stretch out until you're lying straight on top of him, aligned limb to limb. Holding his hands, extend your arms out to the sides and lift the upper body. He keeps his feet flexed so you can push against them with your toes for leverage. Be careful all that body friction doesn't start a fire.

The Buffet

He sits on the floor, his legs spread, with you in his lap facing him and your legs straddling his arms. He then hooks your knees with his elbows and enters you. Thrusting occurs in one of two ways: he can put his hands on your hips and move you or you can lean back on your arms and rock the boat yourself.

The Half Moon

Lie on your side with your upper leg raised. Lying cross-wise to you, your man then inches his body between your open legs – your bodies will now look like an X if seen from above. Once you're joined at the groin, he grabs your shoulders and you anchor on the floor to stabilize each other for a lunar ride.

The Knot

Kneel face to face, then each of you places the same (right or left) and therefore opposite foot flat on the floor and nudges closer, joining genitals. Leaning forward on your planted feet, you rock back and forth for a slow, upright ride to cloud nine.

The Knee-Elbow

Sexier than it sounds, he leans against a wall or a tree. Stand facing him and lift one leg up, supporting your elbows on his. He can then bend down and lift up your other leg. He should keep his movements shallow or you may both fall over.

The Swing

He lies on his back, his legs spread slightly, his head back. Climb on top and literally swing your body forward and backward, pumping the two of you to orgasm.

PENIS PLEASER

Moves you can make during sex that will have his best friend loving you.

- **For ultimate sex**, alternate your mouth with your love organ. Start by lightly sucking him. Then, when he's hard, climb on top and guide him inside. After a few strokes, slip him back inside your mouth. Continue until his earth shakes.

- **Triple whammy** him with loving attention from every angle by putting his penis between your breasts, dipping your head forward to suck the head and using one hand to squeeze the shaft and the other to caress his goodies. (You can keep your breasts in place with your arms.)

- Keep his penile **skin stretched** tight the entire time you are having intercourse by holding it down with your fingers at the base of the shaft. Imagine the heightened sensitivity you would experience if he stretched the skin around your exposed clitoris while thrusting against it with his pelvis and you'll understand why this manoeuvre is likely to send him skyward.

- When he's lying on top of you during sex, get him to spread his legs to take the **pressure off** his testicles. If they're too compressed, they can become over-stimulated and make sex uncomfortable for him although he won't know exactly why. (He'll just think it has something to do with how you make love and won't bother to call again.)

- Lie flat on top of him with your legs in between his and **squeeze your thighs** tightly together – this way you can control how deeply he penetrates you and his penis still gets fully massaged.

- Double his pleasure by turning on his **'G'-spot**. Press on the area between his bottom and his balls with your forefinger during sex until you hit gold.

- Nothing makes his penis happier than sliding inside you as deep as he can. To give him this **deep penetration**, get into missionary position and lift your legs up wide apart. The higher you can go, the further he can thrust – especially if you push into him with each stroke (it helps if you wrap your legs round his shoulders).

- For the same sensation, but even deeper penetration, sit up straight on him during sex, and then **grind your pelvis** slowly round and round and back and forth. At the same time, squeeze your vaginal muscles really tight until you vibrate him up into sex heaven.

FIVE WAYS
OF **BUCKING** HIS BRONCO

Thrusting in and out is all very well. But it could be better. **Much** better.

1. Get him to move his penis from side to side.
A circling action, gradually moving deeper, will have you begging for a replay.

2. Get him to direct his penis up and down.
He can rock your world by bobbing up toward your head and then down toward your bottom. You'll discover all sorts of crackling nerve endings you didn't know existed.

3. Ask him to place a finger in your vagina during penetration.
It'll give you the overwhelming (and totally satisfying) feeling of being completely filled up.

4. Slow his thrusting down.
Once thrusting starts, it's usually over in a matter of seconds. But the faster you both push, the more sensations you miss out on – the feeling of your skin making contact, your breath mingling and, most important, the pleasurable pressure of his penis gradually sinking into you. Take a full minute to perform what you would usually do in just one or two seconds and focus on feeling him move in and out of you moment by moment. The more you can go slo-mo, the more real time orgasms you will have.

5. Take over the thrusting yourself.

Now you can tease him mercilessly. Lower yourself onto his penis but go no further than the very tip of it and then pull off. Repeat nine times. On the tenth, lower yourself all the way down on to his penis, letting it thrust fully into your vaginal canal. Pull yourself back up and begin your next set of attack and retreat, but this time count to eight before dive-bombing for two deep thrusts. Repeat with seven shallow and three deep thrusts and so on. By the time you're due to come in for ten deep thrusts, you'll have lost count.

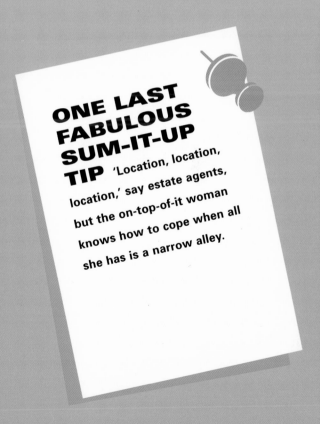

ONE LAST FABULOUS SUM-IT-UP TIP

'Location, location, location,' say estate agents, but the on-top-of-it woman knows how to cope when all she has is a narrow alley.

CHAPTER FIVE ORGASM OR 'FORGET HITHER, JUST COME!'

Come here often?

DID THE EARTH MOVE? IF NOT, WHY THE HELL NOT? GET READY, YOUR NEXT ORGASM IS ABOUT TO HAPPEN. HERE'S HOW TO HAVE BED-ROCKING, PULSE-POUNDING, TOE-CLENCHING, OHMIGOD CLIMAXES EVERY TIME.

HOW TO **HAVE SEX** LIKE A MAN (AND COME EVERY TIME)

This is how he experiences sex: desire, arousal, orgasm. **He sees it, he wants it, he goes for it, he has it.** By rights, you shouldn't be envious – women are capable of multiple orgasms, have more erogenous zones than men and own a sexual organ that exists solely for the purpose of pleasure. All you lack is a little insider info on how to make the most of your stunning attributes.

1. Think about sex.

The average man doesn't need to switch on his sex drive or wait for the mood to strike. He's already in the mood. He's been thinking about sex every waking hour of the day.

2. Decide you want sex and to hell with everything else.

When a man decides to hit the sheets, he doesn't let things like what kind of day he had at the office, how much the scale registered that morning or what the lighting is like get in his way.

3. Don't settle for the almost-but-not-quite experience.

Always expect an earth-moving orgasm. Men don't even consider it sex unless they have an orgasm.

4. Don't subscribe to the cross-your-fingers formula.

Do whatever you need to do to reach orgasm. Guys don't over-analyze or second-guess. If they need porn or extra juice – they just do it. In the same way, tell him what he needs to do to get you off.

5. Don't lose focus by worrying about his pleasure so much.

Believe this: if he needs something, he'll let you know.

6. And this one's tough: fall asleep as soon as you come.

SPOT THE ORGASM

Penis-in-vagina is not exactly what does it for most women. Tongues, hands, fingers and toes all need to be added to the mix. Most of the time. But with a little button-pushing, you can turn intercourse into the never-fail orgasm generator it is for him – without either of you using your hands.

Get to know the exact location of your and his hot spots. (The names aren't sexy but the sensations they generate are.)

Your moan zones

The original C-spot

The clitoris – doh! You know where it is, you know what it's capable of. Now make sure he does!

The G (Grafenberg) spot

A small mass of tissue located inside the vagina, about one third of the way up the front wall. The penis is not the best locating device since it will probably glide past it. He should at first use his middle and index fingers, palms facing him, applying firm pressure until he finds a sensitive place, a patch rougher than the surrounding skin. Bingo.

The AFE (Anterior Fornix Erotic) zone

This is a larger mass of tissue across from the G-spot, on the opposite wall of the vagina. When your AFE area is hit, it can result in waves of muscular contractions that seem hell bent on pushing your lover right out of you. Get him to push back when this happens. The more he pushes into you forcefully, the more intense your pleasure will be.

The U-spot

A tiny area of tissue above the urethra and right below the clitoris.

The new and improved C-spot

A cul-de-sac located near the cervix, this area is only accessible to his penis when the muscles around the uterus lift up as you become extremely aroused. To find your second C-spot, next time you're making love in the missionary position, raise your legs up in the air and move them back toward your body; then suck in your stomach (if you aren't already). These moves should allow his penis access.

His moan zones

Your man has plenty of Big O buttons too. Here are the ABCs to finding his moan zones.

The P-spot

Pressing his prostate, a gland that lies just below his bladder, will make him go wowza. This nerve-rich organ is extremely sensitive and secretes fluid to nourish sperm during ejaculation. Tantalize it by pressing his perineum, that smooth triangle of flesh that lies between the base of his penis and his anus.

The H-spot

The head of his penis is a railroad junction of nerves. Squeeze it and watch him go straight into an orgasmic swoon.

The F-spot

Stroking the frenulum – that loose section of skin on the underside of the penis where the head meets the shaft – will hit his climax switch. Not only are there more nerve endings there, but the skin is also extremely thin.

The R-area

The raphe is the visible seam running up the centre of his scrotum, a generally neglected part of male anatomy. Run your fingertips along it and he may end up ejaculating sooner than he (and you) had planned.

Teach him how to play
Hit the Spot

For a G-spot bull's-eye every time

- Sit on top of him, facing his feet.
- Get on top and lean backward and forward.
- Take it from behind, doggy style.
- Lie on your stomach while he gently lies on top of you so he can penetrate you deeply from behind (you'll get G-spot and clitoral sparks at the same time).
- Lie under him and have him place his hands beneath your hips and lift your whole pelvic area into the air.

Best moves for hitting the AFE zone

- Rear entry.
- Slip a pillow under your hips when you're underneath to tilt your pelvis forward.
- Lie at either the end or side of the bed and have him stand between your legs.
- Get into missionary position and hook your ankles round his shoulders or neck.

Hitting the ultra-sensitive new C-spot

He'll need to go in deep to stimulate this one. Note: these moves are **not for the pregnant** or for diaphragm or IUD wearers (they fit over the cervix).

- Lie on your back with your legs hooked over his shoulders.
- Any rear-entry position.

The Greatest Position in the World

This move manages to hit every single hot spot
ever mapped out by man or woman. Master it to
have a bone-rattling, teeth-chattering, blood-draining,
call-the-medics! orgasm.

1. Stack up a few firm pillows into two piles about 1 m (3 ft) apart.
   Face each other with your backs against the pillows.
2. Connect. It doesn't matter where your arms or legs go – the important
   thing is that your genitals connect. Then lift your hips and/or rotate
   them to experience the full potential of this position.

TIP Clenching your pelvic muscles just
as he pulls out will increase the pressure on
your hot spots and on his.

Synchronized schwinging

Forget the biological clock. Men and women don't even have the same orgasm clock. He seems to come too fast and you seem to come too slow (for each other, that is). It's not important to come together, but something smaller than a London/New York time difference would be nice.

Here's how to re-set your clocks. On your mark... get set... go... oh!

Have him flex his fingers (she speeds up).

Your orgasm is mostly about clitoral stimulation, and his hands offer the most effective way to provide that. Sit on his lap, your back against his chest. He locks his hands in front of you and puts them between your legs. He can then use the middle and ring fingers of one hand to spread your lips gently and slip himself inside you, while using one or two fingers of the other hand to make slow circles round and round your clitoris.

Adjust your legs (she slows while he speeds up).

Get under him and then reposition your legs based on how much speeding up he needs. For more stimulation, lower your knees so that you're lying flat on the bed. He needs still more friction? Close your legs so that his knees are outside yours. You're not likely to orgasm when using either of these variations. But you're also unlikely to lose much ground, arousal-wise.

Use your U-spot (she speeds up).

If you need more time than he does to do what you have come to do, oral sex can give you a head-start before intercourse even begins. Sure, he can focus on your clitoris, but he should also use his lower lip, bracing it against his teeth as he applies apply strong, constant pressure to your U-spot (see page 142).

Thigh thrusts (his 'n her speed ups).

When both of you need a little extra zip in the game, try the 'dual-orgasm position' (or DOG). You raise your right leg until your knee is level with his left shoulder. Your left leg meanwhile still lies flat on the bed. He then directs his thrusts toward the inner thigh of your raised leg. By splitting your legs in this way, you stretch your vagina, allowing for tighter penetration and more pressure on the clitoris. (And if he's ever enjoyed cheerleader fantasies, you'll be his shining star.

Get some rhythm (she speeds up, he slows).

Resist the urge to thrust fast, hard and deep in a standard one-two pattern. Instead, try being more creative: mixing slow, deep thrusts with quick, shallow ones. Start with mostly shallow thrusts that target the first third of your vagina – the most sensitive part – but avoid creating too much stimulation on the head of his penis. Then, as your arousal builds, add a higher ratio of deep thrusts. Try sucking him in slowly and pushing him out quickly – it'll excite your clitoris even more.

Did you say **oh**?

Five tips to help you **come together**.

1. You do your best work when you're on top. But so does he. So to switch positions without losing a beat, lie across the width of your bed instead of the length. If you start near the headboard, you'll have enough room to roll yourselves over completely – down the bed and then back again – as many times as you want.
2. Stop and have him give you a tongue whipping. It'll give his penis a break and send you racing toward the finish line.
3. The longer you spend in one position, the less control you'll have over ejaculation. Try switching from position to position – like window shopping. Return to your favourites, but don't spend more than about thirty thrusts in each one. Chances are, you'll be able to last two or three times longer than normal.
4. Finish doggy-style. This way, you can thrust as much or as little as you need, and as fast or slow as you like. He, meanwhile, is able to change the angle of his dangle to create more friction – remember that downward action will target your G-spot.
5. Educate him – if he learns to recognize when you're getting close to orgasm, he can fine-tune his own pleasure explosion. One of the best ways for him to tell that you're almost there is to listen for the time when your breath becomes short and shallow.

Still single? Learn to multiply

If you can have one orgasm, you can have more than one. And more than one kind. Here's how to distinguish between the different types – a simple guide for those times when one simply isn't enough.

Sequential multiples

These are a series of roller-coaster style climaxes that come fairly close together – from 2 to 10 minutes apart – with a dip in arousal in between. You're most likely to have your boat rocked by sequentials when you have a mouth-sex orgasm followed by an intercourse one.

Serial multiples

In serials the orgasms come one after another, separated by mere seconds with barely any interruption in arousal. Expect these during full-force intercourse as he hits one or more of your hottest spots.

TIP What's the easiest way to keep on coming? Just don't stop. The worst thing he can do to you after you've had one orgasm is: nothing. If your genitals feel too sensitive to touch, try waiting 10 seconds and then restart your engines.

Teach him how to multiply

Men – the poor things – have what's called a 'refractory period'. (In other words, they need a break, and sometimes even a nap, between orgasms.) It doesn't have to be this way. Help him raise his orgasmic threshold by constantly approaching, then – just before he reaches the point of no return – backing away from, ejaculation. Stimulate, then stop and rest; stimulate, then stop and rest. This helps men to separate the sensation of orgasm from the experience of ejaculation. The physical result: he'll now be able to experience all the explosive feelings of orgasm without the ejaculation, again and again and again. The emotional result: he'll adore you forever.

The one-hour orgasm

How to make your orgasm last 60 times longer.

- Take 1 minute to do what you'd normally do in just 2 seconds. Moving in **slow motion** makes you acutely aware of every sensation.

- Straddle him or lie on top, with his penis inside you. He shouldn't move at all; both of you just take time to focus on enjoying the **simple sensation** of containing and being contained – without the extra rush of friction.

- Get him to **stimulate one part** of your body – like the clitoris – until it feels too sensitive, then move to the interior of the vagina until it feels aroused, then return to the clitoris and so on and – sigh – on… You'll have what's called a blended orgasm, a clitoral and vaginal orgasm at the same time, which can last as long as an hour.

- **Tease yourself**. Try to prolong your pleasure by hovering at the brink of orgasm for as long as possible. Build up your arousal and then get your partner to shift his loving attention to a less stimulating part of your body for a few minutes – from your clitoris to your inner thighs or to your breasts maybe, and then return to your clitoris. The beauty of this method is that arousal mounts to such an intensity that when you finally let yourself go, you're practically guaranteed an outrageous orgasm.

Fau**x**gasms

You can't fake happiness, but you **can fake** an orgasm. Do you know why women fake orgasm? Because men fake foreplay.

How to **fool him**

It's been an hour. He's using all his Goalie moves and the only thing happening for you is a numb vagina. You sigh with boredom and he thinks you're enjoying yourself. The sad truth is, short of wiring you to equipment that measures blood pressure, heart rate, vaginal contractions and brain activity, he doesn't have a clue what's going on down there for you. Here's how to put you both out of your misery.

1. Start with a **little moan** (he doesn't need to know it's because your foot is asleep). The female orgasm typically lasts from 6 to 10 seconds (although rolling mega-intense ones can go on for 15 seconds). Clock that. Don't not keep on moaning for half an hour or he will think he has done you serious harm.
2. **Roll your head** from side to side.
3. As you approach 'climax', **increase the tempo** of your movements, particularly of the hips. Make your actions jerky. (Note: If you do not usually move your hips during sex, try it. You may find it affects your arousal so much that you need less faking.)
4. Add 10 seconds of **heavy breathing**.
5. Simulate a slight asthma attack (i.e. **short panting**).
6. **Twitch your vaginal muscles** (don't overdo it – three or four times should do the trick).
7. You might also **arch your back**, scrunch your facial muscles or open your mouth wide.
8. **Collapse** – with a brief 'Oh!' – and let your body go limp with a goofy smile on your face.

TIP Don't be too obvious. Play down the oohs and aahs, and hold off on the whines and tootles, yodels and screeches as your eyeballs disappear in a simulated fog of sexual bliss.

When you **absolutely must** fake it

- Your mother brought you up to be pathologically polite and you think it would be very **rude not to** climax when he's really made such an effort.
- This time you simply can't be bothered to put together the **usual commentary** of 'Not there – there!' and 'Harder, not that hard; higher, no higher'.
- You love him and want to **give him a break** – after all, he's devoted 25 minutes to licking your thighs. It's not his fault that just as you were beginning to lie back and enjoy yourself, you suddenly became aware of a pimple on your chin and now that's all you can concentrate on.
- You gave **at the office** and don't want him to know.
- You know from past experience that he is certain to turn this into an episode of **Goalie sex** if you tell him it isn't going to happen. And that means a night of no sleep and possible tissue damage for you.
- Somewhere between him kissing you like a plunger and then whispering **baby talk** in your ear, you decide this is going to be your first and last time with this guy.

You faked it and now you want to stop.

Sure, once in a while, when you're just not going to get there but normally do, a performance is okay if you feel your lover really needs that. But fake it one too many times and you're stuck since he thinks whatever he is doing works just fine.

There are two things you have to do here.

1. **Wean your lover** off the every-encounter-means-a-big-O you. This means cutting down, not stopping altogether. He's been doing so well up until now, he'll wonder what's going on if you suddenly go cold turkey. Give a stress excuse or whatever but throw in a performance here and there to keep him from guessing. The object is to get him used to the idea that his past techniques aren't quite up to the task now. Hopefully he'll pick up the slack and try new things.

2. Help yourself to have orgasms with your lover by **training him** to give you the sort of orgasms you give yourself when you masturbate. The surest path to orgasmic enlightenment is a little M&Ming (see page 76).

TIP Don't fake it if this is your first time together, you don't like what he is doing and you think you want to see him again. Otherwise, you'll be stuck with his dud moves forever.

How to tell if he's having a mock orgasm

A man can only fake to a certain extent – he can breathe heavily, emit a token grunt and thrust hard. What he cannot do is fake ejaculation, which is an involuntary physical reaction. He will eventually lose his erection but it will take more time than if he really had been shooting bullets.

If you think your partner has pulled a fast one, you can do a **dipstick check**: simply put your finger inside your vagina, withdraw it and take a whiff. Semen has a distinctive smell. If a condom was used and you suspect foul play, you'll need to check that out before he gets rid of the evidence.

You have the power

All it takes is **one small thing** to make your orgasm go boom or bust.

Booms

- Making love on the fourteenth day of your menstrual cycle – that's when the female sex drive is at its highest.
- Going doggy style – you have a better chance of him hitting your G-spot.
- Sex with a curved penis – ditto above.
- Making love a second or third time – you and your body are hot to trot.
- M&M sex – the clitoris is where the action is.
- Fantasizing – this doesn't necessarily mean dreaming of some hottie while your man is covering you with ylang ylang oil (although that never hurts), but rather disconnecting from real life in whatever way works best for you.

Busts

- Tranquillizers, antidepressants, sleeping pills and antihypertensives – all put the sex drive on hold.
- An undiagnosed STI/STD – herpes, chlamydia and other infections can make sex painful (see chapter 8).
- Stress – you can't stop thinking of your finances, those extra 2.25 kg (5 lb) or the fact that your sweet sister is getting married and has picked a dress neatly calculated to make you look just like Little Bo-Peep.
- His (nonexistent) lovemaking skills.
- It's boring – you've read it/seen it/done it/heard it/ dreamed it/bought the T-shirt (twice already).
- Worrying too much how he is enjoying himself.

Emergency

HIM When he's about to come, press firmly with your thumb just below the head of his penis for a few seconds and you've won yourself some catch-up time. YOU Kegels (see page 114) speed things up if you're stuck in third gear.

WHO NEEDS A MAN?

Whether you're in a **long-distance** relationship or **on your own**, you can get by perfectly well without the added testosterone.

Get buzzed

Five reasons why a vibrator is better than a man

1. It's always there when you want it.
2. It never gets tired.
3. It always works.
4. It never wants anything in return.
5. It never asks if you've come.

When a single woman starts buying all the necessities for her first home, it usually involves a trip to the local superstore to get the standards things like blenders, toasters, can openers, coffeemaker, vacuum cleaner, and so on. But vibrators are the **only real must-have** appliance. Think about it – you can get a coffee on your street. But just where are you going to go those times you need an orgasm in a rush?

The clitoris contains 8,000 nerves. At about 2,000 cycles per minute, a vibrator can give your love button the constant stimulation that a hand or tongue cannot adequately provide. It can be downright **addictive**. Experience teaches that it is best to place your vibrator against your skin near the clitoris (but not directly on it, where the sensation can be too intense and even painful). Luckily, there is no any limit to the number of

orgasms you can experience – it isn't as though, for every orgasm you have with your vibrator, you lose one that you could have with your partner.

If you don't have access to a sex shop, you can buy online (all companies offer prompt delivery in discreet brown packaging). Or cheat by getting a battery-powered massager from the pharmacy. Don't worry about the shape – researchers have found that it's the vibrations, not the shape, that triggers orgasm.

Don't scrimp when choosing a model. A good vibrator can be expensive, depending on the material it's made of, or how famous was the porn star whom the advertisers used as a model. The more 'realistic' the feel or the greater the number of added pleasure features, the higher the price. If the price seems a lot, take a moment. You wouldn't think twice about spending a similar amount on a pair of shoes and your vibrator guarantees a lot more pleasure.

TIP Vibrators made of silicone are vastly superior to those constructed from rubber or vinyl – they warm up quickly, retain body heat, are nonporous and easy to clean (more crucial than you'd think). Just like you want him to be able to pass the Sniff Test (see page 174), you don't want to be playing with a funky vibrator.

Babes in Toyland

It's okay to have more tools than the superstore. Just think of it like this. You're not afraid to invest in your own pleasure. You know what you like and how to get off. Anyway, good toys are like chocolates: you can't have just one. If a dozen battery-powered friends are what you need to get you to your happy place, so be it. What's the alternative? Would you rather fake it?

If your partner is so narrow-minded that he sees your toys as stiff competition, ask if his fingers and penis can vibrate at 300 rpm. Then show him that you are good at playing with others and offer to share.

Buzz Off

Little tree-shaped bits and pieces hanging off the top, spurs sticking out of one or both sides... What the hell are those things? Vibrators are not perfect replicas of the penis because, quite frankly, if the penis did it for us, we wouldn't need a vibrator. We could just pick up a banana when no flesh-and-blood model was to hand. Vibrators are shaped the way they are so they can do what the penis can't, and that's hit your clitoris every time. Here are the most popular types.

Plug-in cylindrical

The most popular type of vibrator, these versions have soft, round heads and are closest to resembling a real penis. If you are into accessorizing, some come with a curved attachment that can be used for penetration and G-spot stimulation.

Coil-powered

These look like mini hairdryers but in place of a vent they have a knob. The real advantage to these is that they plug in and run almost silently – perfect if you live in a shared house. They also come with an array of attachments.

Battery-operated

The best ones are the rechargeables that can be used while they are charging. Some are small, portable and waterproof – perfect for the hot tub, bath or shower.

Egg-shaped

Slightly smaller than a real egg, these battery operated gizmos tend to be made of hard plastic that can be inserted into the vagina or held against the clitoris.

Five ways to have an orgasm without a man

1. Sit on anything that vibrates – the spin cycle of the washing machine, the back wheels of a bus, the gearshift of the car.
2. Spread your legs in front of the jet of a jacuzzi.
3. Repeatedly squeeze your vaginal muscles.
4. Ride a horse.
5. Crank up the bass on your sound system.

Rotating, textured shaft

In this somewhat complicated but effective design a rotating shaft vibrates as it turns. The shaft has rolling, textured 'pearls' inside it that feel just lovely at the entrance to your vagina while another part vibrates against your clitoris.

Lipstick

Exactly the same size, shape and even colour as a favourite lipstick, the only difference is that it provides the unexpected bonus of a buzz that can produce amazing results. Bonus: you can leave it lying around since it looks so much like something that belongs in your cosmetics bag.

Miniature

This is a tiny clitoral vibrator that fits over your finger. It's a perfect way to work in a little unobtrusive clitoral stimulation during intercourse with a partner. Note: this works particularly well if you're on all fours or in any other position where one of your hands has a little extra freedom to move against your love button.

TIP Don't get a vibrator that looks like a penis if you intend to share it with your lover – he'll soon be comparing himself (using a tape measure) and wondering if it's his replacement. Very few men are going to be turned on by a moulded plastic facsimile of the real thing that makes them look like a mini.

Pros and Cons

While battery-operated ones are more convenient and less pricey, the plug-ins last longer and vibrate more strongly. It's your call.

Battery-operated models
Often lighter and smaller, they can be packed in an overnight case easily and have no cord to get in the way. They are also less expensive. However, cheaply made ones might not last very long, especially if you use them frequently.

Plug-in models
These are more expensive, but often last longer and have much stronger vibrations. (However, the cord does get in the way a bit.) Plug-in models often come with various attachments that you can place over the head, many of which can be used on tired feet and aching backs as well.

TIP The secret to getting the biggest buzz is to back off on the pressure, keep the vibrator moving and avoid direct contact with your clitoris.

Pleasure junkies
You know you're hooked on your vibrator when:

- You'd rather masturbate than catch up on the latest *Sex and the City* tape.
- You have a panic attack when you're down to your last two batteries.
- You can replace the dead batteries in the dark.
- You don't care if your boyfriend is late.
- The power goes down and the first thing you think about is your vibrator.

Virtual sex

Cybersex. Where else can a fat, balding 50-year old bachelor tell everyone he is really 'rugged gd. looks, powerful build, tall, broad-shouldered'? Or even 'Fifi', a statuesque Las Vegas showgirl? One of the greatest attractions of cybersex is that you can be anyone you want to be and say anything you want to say.

It's common for cybersexers to assume **different personalities**, or to invent idealized portraits. Fantasies are, after all, the stuff that cybersex is made of (or perhaps the magnetic rays from monitors are causing men's genitals to mutate to a standard XXL).

Cybersex is free, on call 24 hours a day, seven days a week, and it's interactive, with a real person on the other end. **Safer than a one-night stand**, you don't even have to dress to come to the party.

Cyber rules

If **virtual sex** isn't something you do with your lover, then make sure you are alone before logging on. Think about it: won't it get really difficult explaining what you are doing undressing in front of the computer, drooling out of one corner of your mouth, moaning and groaning, all to the accompaniment of various buzzing 'toys'?

1. Make sure that your computer doesn't plant 'cookies' or the next person to log on is going to know just exactly where you've been.
2. No matter what you are truly wearing (sweatpants, sweat shirt, torn bathrobe, slippers, T-shirt with stains on the front, baggy underwear), always tell your potential cyber partner you are wearing a thong, garter-belt with black stockings, stilettos and a 34DDD bra.
3. When things start steaming, check your spelling before you send that embarrassing typo, e.g., 'I just love your hot, wet silly'; 'Oh baby, you have such a big coke' (hope you got the supersized fries and burger with that); 'Oh fork me hard!'.
4. Pay attention to what's going on. That way you'll refrain from asking your cyberpartner to put his 'coke' in one place, when he's just typed that it was someplace else.

5. Do not fake a cyberorgasm. If the cyber is not going well, let the other person know in the best way you can. Here are some suggestions.

- You suddenly have this burning need to get a manicure (so what if it's only 3 am?).
- Tell him your lover just walked in and you have to log off.
- Weird him out – say that you can only orgasm if he'll describe himself taking a dump.
- Say you have to let your dog out.
- Or if you really want to hit him below the belt – type that you are just not feeling this.

TIP Never give out any personal info online like your full name, where you live, where you work, what your phone number is, credit card numbers and so on. The reason? You don't want people infiltrating your life in case they turn out to be psychos or you get bored. Always sign on with a screen name so you can quickly fade it after the encounter if you want (or need) to.

Phone sex: seven rules for getting started

Phone sex is fantastic for a woman on-the-go. Next time you're aching for some extra attention or just a thrill, call him (it can be even better if you misdial).

1. Keep a sexy magazine on hand in case you get dry-mouth.

2. Whisper or talk in a husky voice. What you say matters less than how you say it. 'I love scrambled eggs' can sound sexy in a soft, throaty tone.

3. Play 'See Jane Run'. Tell him in simple sentences what you are doing as you are doing it – 'I am playing with my left nipple. It's getting hard. It's making me squirm...' You get the idea.

4. Speak the same language. If he says, 'pussy' and that makes you steam in a way unintended or you say 'big one-eyed friend' and that makes him giggle, you are not going to get anywhere.

5. Keep talking. If you're finding it hard to produce sentences complete with subject and verb, nouns and articles, make noise – moan, sigh loudly, grunt, throw in a few yeses and pleases. Cry his name. Ask him what he wants or how he feels.

6. Still tongue-tied? Read a sexy passage from that mag or a book.

7. If you still have lockjaw, e-mail him.

ONE LAST FABULOUS SUM-IT-UP TIP

When you want to come to the party, supply your own ride. Remember that sex is an acquired skill, but masturbation comes naturally.

CHAPTER SIX MIND YOUR MANNERS
OR 'NEVER PAY THE BILL IF THE DATE WAS BAD'

For men, **sex** is like a bank account. Once he **withdraws,** he loses interest.

HERE'S HOW TO GET HIM OUT OF YOUR PLACE AFTER A ONE-NIGHT STAND OR FIGURE OUT WHEN IT REALLY IS CHEATING. GUIDELINES FOR THE GAME WHERE THERE'S ZERO PREDICTABILITY, NO REFEREE AND EVERYONE IS PLAYING BY THEIR OWN SYSTEM.

SANITIZED SEX

Women are considerate enough to do away with their body hair, make sure their garden literally smells like flowers, and keep their breath pleasantly fresh to be certain that they and their partners will have a good time. When are men going to accept that they should reciprocate the favour?

Funky smells

Toilet breath

It's one thing to **taste yourself** when your honey kisses you, but what if it tastes like someone died in your sweetie's mouth? Do you say anything? We all have stinky breath once in a while, so there's no need to make a fuss if it's the odd occurrence. But if it's chronic and you don't want to talk about it, you had better start carrying breath mints.

TIP Slip into something sexy and 69ish right after popping a breath mint – it is guaranteed to add a lovely tingly zest to your mouth action.

Bad BO

Hot and sweaty after sex is good, but before is another matter altogether. You are not doing him any favours by letting him wander around smelly all day.

TIP Make taking a shower together part of foreplay. Lather him up and then rinse him off.

Passing the Sniff Test

We all have our own, **unique bouquet**. Unfortunately, some guys think all women should smell like roses. Get to know your scent like a long-time friend (this way you'll know whether it's his hang-up or if there is a real problem –

intense aromas can signal that you have an infection or STI/STD). Be aware of how your scent changes depending on how horny you are or whether you are about to drop an egg (when your smell may be stronger to attract mates and your vagina may produce more mucus to protect and guide sperm on its way to your uterus… ah, mucus, so sexy, so alluring!).

You can't do much about the havoc that hormones wreak on your body, but there are some preventative measures to keep you smelling like you're supposed to (and that's not like a daisy or a summer's breeze).

- **You reek what you eat.**
  Too much sugar, caffeine, refined carbohydrates, red meat, alcohol or nicotine can give you a slightly off odour (and flavour). Eat right and your partner will be more into eating you.

- **Ditch the leather pants.**
  Tight clothing (especially tight Lycra when you're working out) and synthetic underwear can stop air circulating down there, creating the perfect, moist environment for bacteria to over-grow. So either indulge his white cotton brief fantasy or sleep naked.

- **Don't stress. Get rest.**

- **Wash behind your lips every day.**
  That means the whole shebang (backdoors and front). However, don't douche – it can cause infections.

- **Wipe after you go the bathroom.** You'd be surprised...

- **Avoid deodorizing products.** Deodorized or scented anything is usually a bad idea down there: tampons, pads, potpourri sachets, candles and so on. But frankly, a spritz of perfume never hurt anyone.

TIP If you're not sure whether you smell sweet, stick your hand down your pants and sniff your fingers.

- **He's shooting sour milk.** A man's semen can run the gamut from sweet to bitter, fresh to fishy depending on what he ate that day. Eating fruit, especially pineapple and apples, is supposed to make sperm sweeter. Some bad smells could be a sign of infection, especially if his penis is grungy looking.

TIP If he refuses to believe he is anything but willy-luscious, challenge him to sample some of his own output. If he's okay with it, then you probably will be too. However, if he chokes it down like a man forced to eat live worms, it's time for him to change his diet.

Accidental (hopefully) farting

If you let **one slip**, chances are he won't care. Men tend to be a lot less squeamish about body functions than women (must be all that peeing together). But if you feel you must acknowledge your indiscretion, you can try blaming the dog (which obviously only works if there really is a canine in your bedroom and that would have to beg the question: why?). Otherwise, try a little comic relief: 'Wow, you're good – you knocked the wind right outta me.' Or you can divert his attention by talking up his prowess between the sheets. Say he's going down on you at the time – tell him, 'Keep going. Just lift your head, take a breath of air and then keep doing exactly... oh!... what... you're... doing... aaah!'

TIP If he lets one go during the act, just ignore it and breathe through your nose for a while.

Varting in bed

When your vagina makes like a **whoopee cushion** during sex, it means air was pushed into your vagina (often the result of a lot of intense thrusting), and is now leaking out. It's not dangerous, but neither is it exactly sexy. Here's how to avoid the dreaded vaginal deflation.

- **Add more grease.**
  Lubrication makes everything **slick**, so as the penis moves it can't create air pockets.
- **Try woman on top.**
  These positions make for a tighter seal and let in less air (rear entry seems to build up your vaginal air supply).
- **Change position during sex.**
  It may reduce the air pressure and give any air that's built up a chance to escape discreetly.

TIP Don't stress – at least they don't smell.

You need a haircut

Pubic hair in teeth is one of the more unpleasant side effects of oral sex. Both men and women should show consideration by managing their forests. You don't have to clear all vegetation – a little trim should do the job. Some men report they find it easier to perform major tongue action when they have fuzz-free access.

Body blunders

HER BIGGEST GROSS OUT

- You make love, assume that he got rid of the condom and then put your bare foot on something **cold and slippery** the next morning.
- Or you discover it days later next to the bed.
- Or (worst) your mother finds it on one of her unannounced snooping visits.

It doesn't take a brain surgeon to figure out that a used condom belongs in the trash. Men need to learn to be Spill Masters. You're not his mother – it's his responsibility to throw the condom out post-sex.

HIS BIGGEST GROSS OUT

- **Period** sex

Guys will put up with a lot to get down and dirty, but many start making the sign of the cross at the concept of period sex, convinced that the post-coital embrace will resemble something out of *Texas Chain Saw Massacre*.

The reality is that the **total fluid** is only a couple of tablespoons. To keep any mess to a minimum, avoid your heavy days and simply have sex in the shower. Wet and squishy is wet and squishy. Period! Or make your vagina a blood-free zone by using a diaphragm or cap to hold back the flow while you get horizontal.

For oral sex, you can wear a tampon but remove it if you're moving on to the next level – it could become lodged inside you and you'll require a doctor's help to remove it.

TIP Frankly, whatever his feelings on the subject, you want to have sex right now. Many women are at their horniest when they're bleeding because there's an increased blood flow to the pelvis (engorgement is an orgasm's secret ingredient). But let him know what time of the month it is or he'll think he's been castrated when he sees his penis covered in blood. Best moment to come clean is when the clothes hit the floor – he's usually so focused on what's coming next by then that he probably wouldn't care if you said you had two vaginas.

ALERT! You can still get pregnant during your period.

Health and safety

- Lock up any animals. Draw the line at anything that does not live in a tank.
- Ditch the chewing gum.
- If you sneak off for a quickie handjob or a blowjob and don't swallow, make sure he doesn't leave any blobs on you.

SEX PLAY

His biggest cock-ups and how to fix them

COCK-UP 1: HE'S SUFFOCATING YOU.

Okay, he's practically suffocating you, he's pressing so hard. Or you're giving him a blowjob and he is stuffing himself so far down your throat that you are about to gag. How long should you keep it up before you truly need to worry about passing out?

FIX-IT Keep going until he stops. Do come up for air, but think about how you would feel if he stopped before you were ready: let down? angry? Ready to sob, scream and swear.

COCK-UP 2: HIS DICK IS FLOPPY.

When a man has shrivelled up, his Y chromosome (as in, 'Y me? Y now?') can infuse him with self-blame and shame. Three terrible concerns loom larger and larger in his mind: **1.** He is a failure, **2.** He has let you down, or **3.** You are going to tell all your friends about this.

FIX IT Forget talking, especially patronizing lines like, 'Don't worry – it happens to everyone.' What does he care about everyone? So ignore his flop and keep moving. Bump and grind here; guide his hand there... and then come on home. That's right. Have an orgasm. Some fondling can't hurt. Don't rush – you're not trying to make the last train – just do some subtle stroking and climb around a little. Your moans of delight will bolster his confidence – with luck, as his ego re-inflates, so will his other body parts.

COCK-UP 3: HE'S HURTING YOU.

He's shipped out his (self) acclaimed super-duper-ten-orgasms-guaranteed move and the only thing it seems to be giving you is pain with every thrust.

FIX IT If the words, 'Er, that sort of hurts' are too hard to utter, try a subtler approach: say, 'You know what I love?' and move yourself into a position that gives you more control over the speed and angle. He'll never suspect anything was wrong. So if he is pinning you to the mattress during missionary, give a gentle push on his shoulders until you've flipped over and you're on top. If he does something you really hate, like sucking your belly button, saying, 'That isn't one of my hot spots, but down here is' will be more effective than shouting, 'Get out of my navel, you lint muncher!'

COCK-UP 4: HE CAME; YOU DIDN'T.

The cold hard truth is that he has zero concern in your orgasm once he's done with his. It's not that he doesn't care about you. But it's a well-known biological fact that after a man opens and shoots, his raging lust converts to an insatiable urge to pass out.

FIX IT You have four options when you miss his pleasure cruise (choose whichever suits you best).

- The dominatrix: 'What? You're finished? No way – get back in there, bucko!'
- The flatterer: wait a few minutes, snuggle up and, kissing him, gently place his hand where you want it, sighing, 'More, please.'

- The sex babe: 'Could you keep pleasuring me – that feels really good and I'm not quite finished yet.'
- The guilt inducer: keep going on your own. Hopefully, he'll feel left out and it won't be long before his ego will force him back into the action.

The point is: if you stop, it's a sign to him that you're satisfied. And you're clearly not. But you could also get your orgasm in first. Casually tell him it's a little known fact that while very few women see stars during intercourse almost all women climax from oral sex.

COCK-UP 5: HE WANTS TO KEEP ON GOING AND YOU WANT TO GO TO SLEEP.

The `I don't want you' dilemma is tough. Personal rejection – and it doesn't get more personal – is always upsetting. But no way should you spread your legs and risk a Soregasm if you'd rather be clipping your toenails.

FIX IT Do what he always does – avoid the whole issue by pretending to be asleep.

Dirty talk

Could you please just shut up already?

Mummy, dearest

While in the throes of **passion**, he yells out, 'Yes, Mummy! Yes, Mummy!' Hopefully, he is shouting 'Yes, Mummy!' the same way some men shout 'Oh, baby!' Still, sexy it's not. Tell him to can the mummies and insert your name instead.

TIP When a man has a real problem with his mother, you will notice it in the way he lives his life – calling her every day, depending on her to wash his clothes and make dinner for him, comparing everything you do to She Who Gave Birth To Me And Is So Marvellous – not in what he whispers in your ear when you are playing sheet music.

He's a howler

While it's **nice to know** when he is about to come, it's not so nice to be with a guy who shouts so loud that he alerts the rest of the world to his orgasmic status.

You could make him feel self-conscious about his mating calls by asking him if he hurt himself. Or appeal to his chivalrous side and tell him your housemate/landlord/neighbours are threatening to evict you because they're convinced you have begun practising black magic.

TIP Check if the noises seem to get worse during each full moon.

Oral sex talk

He **talks incessantly** during sex. Worst of all, he asks you to describe how you're feeling every second. Or right after, asks, 'Am I the best you've ever had?' This is a man who needs to have his ego rather than his penis stroked during sex. Sighing and moaning might shut him up, but he's more likely to ask what it is he is doing that is making you purr like a kitten.

Since you can't exactly hit a mute button, try drowning out his voice with some sexy background music. Or tell him that sex is a religious act for you and you would appreciate a moment of silence.

TIP Give the guy a little credit. Chances are he's just trying to figure out the lay of the land and is overly eager to please you.

Shut your mouth

Quick recoveries for bad language in the heat of passion

You cried, 'I love you' in the middle of an orgasm.
There's a tactic understanding that any 'I love yous' blurted in the middle of sex don't count. Still, even 'I love yous' understood to be accidental will give him the upper hand. Continuing to talk will make your slip-up seem less important than if you instantly shut up, clasp your hands over your mouth and give him an 'I can't believe I said that' panic gaze. Two solutions that rarely fail:

- **I love you... 'to do that' or 'to touch me there'.**
  Pretend to be so overcome with passion that you can't manage good grammar.

- **'Stick it to me, big boy, you are so big, oh boy.'**

  His head will swell so much that he won't even
  remember what you said first.

You called out the wrong name.

Early in the game, screaming the wrong name in the heat
of passion is a little more excusable. If, however, you're
into year two or three of the relationship, you'd better have
a good excuse or a comfy couch. One quick recovery is to
pretend you were comparing him with an old lover (with him
coming out on top, of course): 'Oh, Tom, Tom, my ex Tom
used to do that but nowhere near as good as you.'

TIP It might not be a bad idea to follow this up by
shouting his name ten times at the top of your voice.

YOU BLURT:	IMMEDIATELY CONTINUE WITH:
'Oh god, my ex used to do that!'	'...oh god, sex like that, oh!'
'Is it in?'	'...uh-incredibly big?'
'Do you love me?'	'...to give you a blowjob?'

You said something embarrassing when talking dirty.
Talking dirty is an acquired art, like rapping or writing bad poetry. Any mention of parents, peeing or gang-banging will leave him cold. If you come out with something you immediately regret, move on as quickly as possible. Dwelling on it will only make it worse.

TIP Stick with what he's doing at this moment in time.

Passing the oral exam

Q: How do you make a vagina talk?
A: Put a tongue in it!

Q: What do I do if I'm scared of gagging?
A: Your gag reflex will kick in if his penis – or a gush of ejaculate – hits the back of your throat unexpectedly. So, rather than taking him head on, try sucking his dangle at a slight angle – perhaps into your cheek. This way, if he spurts, you'll just end up looking like a squirrel for a moment or two (which, let's face it, really is much sexier than a full-throttle, coughing, semen-spewing fit).

If you absolutely refuse to swallow, at least be nice about it. Don't spit it out very obviously and sprint to the bathroom to gargle.

TIP A WET-SPOT QUERY: What is the proper procedure after he deposits his load somewhere other than your mouth or vagina? Generally, he should offer to wipe up if he's given you a pearl necklace.

Q: How can I cope if he's too XL for my mouth?

A: An oversize can present as much of a problem as a mini. But there are ways to make his mammoth member easier to take, depending on whether he's too wide or too long (or even, bless you, both).

Just as you (hopefully) would if you were trying to accommodate him during intercourse, get super-wet. Try holding a few teaspoons of water in your mouth for extra lubrication. (Note: cold water may shrink him a bit.) He'll love the slick feeling.

TIP You don't have to eat his entire penis. The head is the most sensitive part, so just lick and suck the tip while using your hands to stroke along his shaft. Pretend your hands are an extension of your mouth and have them work in tandem.

Q: Dick breath. Discuss.

A: Many men like to joke that they'd give themselves oral sex if they could, but for some kissing your mouth after it's been kissing his penis is akin to coming out. Chances are these guys are not so into sharing the wealth. If he doesn't seem to enjoy kissing after you've been snacking, give your mouth a wipe on the sheets. Then slowly work your way back up, kissing his chest, neck, chin, ears.

TIP If he's bothered by his own secretions, he's probably not going to be overly fond of yours.

Q: Why is he into douche sex?

A: After oral sex, does he catapult out of bed in a manner that suggests, 'I must sterilize ASAP' before your orgasmic contractions have even stopped? If he has fluidphobia, then sex with him is always going to make you feel like Swamp Woman. Your call.

But he has two possible excuses. **1.** He may be reacting to your taste. Stick with him a month since your body fluids change depending on what you eat and your hormonal cycle. If he's more inclined to cuddle certain times, you may want to think about your diet. **2.** It could be an STI/STD (see pages 240–47) and you may need to get checked out.

Q: What do I do if he takes ages to come?

A: If you feel like it's been so long since you've come up for air that the hair has regrown on your legs, it's time to speed things along. Try switching from stimulation by mouth to doing it by hand – and then apply more pressure to the bottom of the shaft of his penis, and to his testicles.

TIP Try not to yawn.

Q: How do you handle a Vagitarian?

A: If only all men would realize that oral sex is your get-out-of-the-doghouse-free card (although Manolo Blahnik shoes also do in a pinch). If he absolutely refuses to kiss your other lips, then give him the kiss off. Sure, you may be able to teach him new tricks. But you would always be wondering if he felt in desperate need of a toothbrush and what does that do for your orgasm?

Don't try these at home

Men are not **like dogs** – they're more like paranoid
puppies. That's why they tend to have such bad lovemaking
manners. Here are some of their more frequent trip-ups.

- **Helping her take her clothes off more quickly.**
  It's his idea of 'foreplay'.

- **Taking etiquette advice from porn movies.**
  In X-rated films, women love it when men ejaculate
  over them. In real life, it just means more laundry.

- **Attempting sex and saying it was an accident.**
  Outside the kitchen, this is how men earn a reputation
  for not being able to follow directions. If he wants to put
  it there, he should ask first.

- **Nudging her head down.**
  Men persist in doing this until you're eyeball-to-penis,
  hoping that it will lead very swiftly to mouth-to-penis. All
  women hate it. It's about three steps from being dragged
  to a cave by your hair. If he wants you to use your mouth,
  he should use his – and talk seductively to you.

- **Needing a map-reading course.**
  It's the only part that protrudes. How hard is that?

- **Eating the hole.**
  The hole does not bring pleasure, the clitoris does. It's
  like you spent the evening playing with his pubic hair.

THE MORNING AFTER

There are basically **two kinds** of one-night stands – the nameless-fuck thing or the scratching-an-itch-with-a-friend thing. If you want to walk away afterward with no strings attached, go with the nameless fuck. However, if you are looking for an occasional sure-thing fling for your horny times of the month when you're between men, you may be better off finding yourself a regular Fuck Buddy.

Nine ways to have a great one-night stand

One-night stands tend to be super-charged sexual chemistry sessions or sad, drunken fumbles because you missed the last ride home. Make sure yours is the former.

1 It's best not to go to your usual stomping ground – think of it as not peeing in your own backyard. It also helps edit out **potential stalkers**.

2 **Be prepared.** Don't be too hairy and make sure you have condoms in your handbag.

3 Choose **your partner** wisely. Pick a man you think is sexy. Why waste this experience on someone mediocre just because he happens to be there?

4 Drink – in **moderation**. One or three drinks will lower inhibitions and help keep the mood. Too many and you will perform like a wet sponge. Think of it as maintenance – one before you go home together, one when you get home.

TIP It's easy to end up Retro-Dating a one-nighter if you can't remember anything about the night. One too many Cosmopolitans have been responsible for more badly-made-matches in lovers' land than your Great Aunt Gertrude.

5 **Don't start lying** – not only will he like to know this is just sex, nothing more, it will take a lot of the crap out of his sails as you won't have to listen to him planning his escape without you twigging. Mention another man you still love – your husband, boyfriend, ex. Or that you are leaving town the next day... permanently. Do and say nothing that makes him think you want to see him again.

6 Now is the time to be **sexually selfish**. You want one thing – an orgasm (well, perhaps a few things). Make him work harder than you've ever had anyone work before. It's about time all that jaw-aching oral sex resulted in something more than a snoring body on the other half of the bed. Be bossy – demand and bark until you are yelping and moaning. Remember, you aren't doing it to entice or keep your lover – you are getting a need fulfilled and that's it. Bite, scratch, spank, get sweaty and savour it. Screw appearances and social expectations – you're here to get your groove on first.

7 Say everything you've ever wanted to say in bed but were too afraid. Harder, faster, invoke old lovers, movie stars, hell, even cartoon characters, if it turns you on. Claw out that orgasm with a frenzy you've held back in the name of civility during your relationships.

TIP At the same time, keep it courteous! There is no excuse for rudeness, even if you suspect this guy may be an asshole. Call it karma, kismet or coincidence, what you do now may come back to haunt you later.

8 Don't look back – the worst thing you can do is feel guilty or disgusted or act if you wish you were elsewhere. You're here, sex is on the table, you might as well get into it and make it good sex.

9 Use a **condom**. Again, **USE A CONDOM**. It's the worst time to get pregnant – you already know you don't want to spend the rest of your life with this man. Also, you don't know him – so there's no way you have any idea what nasty germs might be dwelling in his nether regions.

TIP If you did forget to suit him up – or you just can't remember whether you did or not – you may want emergency protection such as the post-coital pill (aka the morning-after pill) to be on the safe side (see chapter 7 for details).

EMERGENCY ESCAPE PLAN You and a tall, dark and handsome connect and slip off to your place for a night of passion. But when he **kisses you**, his tongue darts in and out like a frightened minnow while his lips tense into a frozen O and your only thought is, 'How the hell do I get this guy out of here?'

There is no way to explain such a sudden change of heart. At a loss for words (other than, 'Wow, that kiss was really awful, there is no way I can go on!'), you can try throwing a Bit Flip. Mumble how you aren't really ready for this, you feel very vulnerable and it wouldn't be fair to him, yadda yadda. Or else fake a sudden migraine. Or remember that you have to be somewhere else in 5 minutes. You could tell him you just got your period and need to get some tampons but he may be willing to wait.

DRASTIC MEASURE Say you forgot you're having a herpes or genital warts flare-up.

TIP Don't ever slip off with someone until you've kissed.

Post-sex protection

Let's face it. No one's going to be calling anyone. And you both have morning-after booze breath strong enough to take an eye out. So lose the pretence. It's probably best not to spend the night together as you risk hearing his bodily functions and that can ruin everything. So here's what do you do with him when it's over.

Spending the night at his place

You might think a dream date for your average man is a lover who flees without a trace. But, in practice, they have feelings, too. They think, 'What, no quick peck goodbye on the forehead? No short but sweet note left on my pillow? No generous tip on the nightstand?' So don't sneak out in the middle of the night.

ESCAPE PLAN 1 A simple, 'Thanks, that was fun, nice to meet you, take care,' will suffice. Throw in a hug if you simply can't be that nonchalant.

ESCAPE PLAN 2 Say, 'I've had a beautiful time, but I have to get up really early for work (if it's a weekday)/because my boyfriend is coming over (if it's a weekend).'

When he spends the night at your place

It's harder to get someone to leave than to leave yourself. You need to be tough and think of yourself as a bartender during last call: 'C'mon, let's go. You don't have to go home but you can't stay here!' What do you do if he walks out? Sweet thing, you just close the door.

EJECTION PLAN 1 Walk towards the door saying, 'I've got a brutal day tomorrow, and if you're here, I'll want to stay up all night.'

EJECTION PLAN 2 Get up and hit the shower, saying, 'Don't worry about locking the door.' He'll take the hint.

EJECTION PLAN 3 For a classy **shove out the door**, get up, give him coffee in bed (so he doesn't fall asleep), and then make him a great snack. After you have finished eating, say you called a taxi for him, but that it won't be there for an hour (giving you the opportunity for one last session of monkey love).

EJECTION PLAN 4 If the sex was bad and you want him out fast, throw his jeans at his head and say, `Later, Tiny.'

EJECTION PLAN 5 Say your boyfriend will be home soon (add, 'from kickboxing class' if you really want to see him fly).

EJECTION PLAN 6 Say you own a Debbie Gibson CD and you're not afraid to use it.

ALL PURPOSE LINE WHEREVER YOU END UP
You have to get up early the next morning.

Whussisname?

You wake up and you have no idea who is sleeping next to you. Don't panic.

If you're at his place

Look for clues. His name has to be somewhere – on the pretext of going to the bathroom scan the medicine cabinet for any prescriptions with his name, check if there are magazines with subscription labels, take a peek in the trash bin to see if there is any thrown-away post.

If you're at your place

You could try peeking into his wallet when he is in the bathroom, but it's probably more embarrassing to be caught rifling through his things than admitting temporary amnesia.

Trick him into revealing it

You could ask if he ever had a nickname or if he's named after someone in his family. Then again, you could just not bother if you don't plan to see him again anyway.

TEMPORARY MEASURE Use some generic name: sweetie, love, darlin' are all acceptable substitutes.

You have a re-run

You spend the night with a co-worker, fellow student or someone who's always in your local bar. Chances are you're going to see them around sometime or other. Here's how to deal when you bump into your one-nighter.

Co-worker

You must be able to face each other at the water cooler. If you are not interested in dating him in the least, you need a strong closing storyline. Kiss him goodnight and say, 'Thanks for a fun evening. I just broke up with my boyfriend and I was feeling really down. Now I know I can deal with dating again.' He ends up feeling flattered that he was able to be your Superman and is less likely to notice that you have just given him a brush-off.

When you do see him, if he acts awkward, put him at ease by saying, 'Thanks for the other night – I really needed that' (this must be accompanied by a quick exit or you put yourself at risk of getting a repeat request).

Leftover sex

So your ex-boyfriend/-lover/-partner doesn't think you are planning a rematch, say, 'That was stupid of us' and then, instead of spending a useless evening rehashing your relationship and discussing why it didn't work out for the two of you, make a quick exit.

TIP If an ex calls, it usually means his hand is tired.

Near stranger

Unfortunately not strange enough – you met through mutual friends and will definitely meet again. Since he is mates with a bunch of your mates, you want to keep this on friendly terms (and make sure he doesn't blab to his friends). The best bet is to be flippant – say, 'Hey, how's it going? Had any good one-night stands lately?'

You hang out at the same places but don't mix

Customize any of the following for an approach that you are going to feel comfortable with:

- **Joke** 'Excuse me, don't I know you?'
- The Obvious and Therefore **Funny Lie**: 'Sorry I haven't been in touch. I'm training for the space programme.'
- The **Cold-Blooded** Move: Pretend you don't know him.

THE **CHEATING** PARADOX

General rule of thumb… or penis… or clitoris is: if you have to ask if it's cheating, then it probably is. You don't have to be swapping body fluids. If you don't want to tell your boyfriend whassup, then you might as well be body bumping.

What's the score?

RATING

☆ You have nothing to hide.

☆☆ You're on the edge.

☆☆☆ Make sure you shower before you get together with your regular.

Double Dipping ☆

No long-term commitments or promises have been made (right?). So it's okay to window shop when dating as long as neither guy is under the impression that he is your one and only. This doesn't mean telling all (unless asked, of course). BUT, telling him that you both should see other people is practically an announcement that you have somebody waiting in the wings.

TIP You will need to keep track of your players' names. Nothing deflates the male ego (and related parts) faster than having a stranger's name moaned into his ear in a moment of passion. And you'll have to be absolutely scrupulous in your safe-sex practices; you may be doubling your pleasure, but you're also doubling your risk.

You're in an open relationship ☆

If you are both agreed on the nature of your relationship, then you can never cheat – as long as you don't pull a Double Whammy. There are three implicit rules of friendship: **1.** You don't fuck your friends' boyfriends/girlfriends, **2.** No, seriously, you don't ever fuck your friends' boyfriends/girlfriends, and **3.** You have to help them move.

Fantasizing about someone else ☆

Salivating over someone other than your main man – even during sex – is totally fine. That is, unless you can't get hot and horny with your guy unless you start playing your own special movie over in your head. In which case, you might want to ditch the current man and find someone who is better at fulfilling your dreams.

TIP The key is just not to shout 'Give, it to me, Brad!' when his name's actually Dennis.

You're more than two time zones apart ☆

You can assume you are in an open relationship if you don't see each other more than once a month.

Phone sex ☆☆

While phone sex can be all you have if you are in a long-distance relationship, this is also the easiest sort of cheating there is. Think – no evidence other than high phone bills. Which means if he's doing it with you, he maybe doing it with other women as well.

Cliterature ☆☆

Hardcore porn tends to be more of a **male fixation**. If he is into it, then he is fixating on a standard you could never attain without implants, a personal trainer, soft lighting, a squad of make-up artists and hairdressers, and airbrushing. So you have the right to be pissed. But is it cheating? It depends. If it's an occasional thing that he pulls out and plays a solo song to, then it may just be a maintenance orgasm – him scratching a distracting physiological itch. But if he is hiding his triple X library and masturbating to the point where he is too worn out to do it with you, it's cheating. You have every right to leave him to his paper dolls and his right hand. He's not worth the trouble.

Doing it online with someone else ☆☆

The cyber-partner is always going to be better than the real flesh-and-blood guy because he can **fulfil all your needs** with a click of his mouse. The anonymity allows you (and your virtual lover) to present yourselves as people you're not, but may have always wanted to be.

You have a last-minute fling ☆☆

Is it cheating? Yes, but it's **good cheating**. Last-minute flings are a good way to tell how you feel before you take the next permanent step. A sort of naked coin toss. The benefit is that it helps you make up your mind and prevents you from being unfaithful later when the stakes are higher (e.g., you've underwritten his business loan).

You have Leftover Sex ☆☆ (☆ possibly)

There are three kinds of ex sex – last-hurrah sex, bad-idea sex which just proves once and for all that he's a fuckface, and out-of-loneliness and weakness sex. If you are already in a relationship, the first two are bumps in the road of proving to yourself that your break is permanent and unlikely to happen again. So they don't really count as cheating. However, the last kind suggests that you are not really as happy-go-lucky in your current relationship as you may have thought you were. In which case, there is only one way to cure your craving for a leftover roll in the hay and that is to fire your current replacement and get a new one until you can stand (or lie) on your own two feet.

You are having a long-term affair. ☆☆☆

Long-term affair: do you really need to ask?

When cheating works for you... and when it doesn't

IT'S A GOOD THING WHEN...	KEEP YOUR KNICKERS ON IF...
You're unhappy with your relationship but too lazy to do anything about it. Cheating can give you that necessary shove to move on and stop wasting both your lover's and your own time.	You are drunk. Let's face it: you can't even put your lipstick on straight when you're trashed, let alone make a decision that could knock the stuffing out of your current relationship.
You need to be reminded of what you do have. When you're in a relationship for a long time, you can't help but start taking your significant other for granted. Sometimes you feel the passion or romance is gone or you forget just how great the man you have really is. Sleeping with some poor schlub can be an insta-reminder.	You are in a grass-is-always-greener-on-the-other-side mood. If worries that you will regret all the guys you missed out on when you break up with your current beau (which has about a 95 per cent chance of happening) lead you to cheat, chances are you will end up confessing all, your boyfriend will dump you and you will immediately realize he's The One and Only.

Your sex life is DOA. You've tried lingerie, you've tried 'going commando', you've raided the fridge and done everything short of twisting yourself into knots to turn him on. Sometimes, you need a jump in the sack with something willy-luscious to help you figure out if the lack of orgasms in your life is due to you, your boyfriend or the (lack of) chemistry between you.

You're in lust. But once you cheat, guaranteed you will lie in bed racked by feelings of guilt and fear. Because, as your head clears you'll find that your fling often doesn't measure up to that fabulous fantasy. Now you remember the good reality: the man who loves you, fixes the plumbing and makes love to you. The old saying 'you don't know what you've got till it's gone' says it all.

Men who don't count as cheat material

- When you have revenge sex (he cheated on you so now you get your own back)
- Anyone bad in bed
- When you're drunk and can barely remember it
- Vacation flings
- Mercy sex: his girlfriend dumped him
- When you want to stop counting

Rules to cheat by

How to get away with Double Dipping without getting your stiletto permanently imbedded in your skull.

RULE 1: KEEP YOUR LIES SIMPLE.

Telling your boyfriend that you need to put in extra time at work to get a project done will buy you some late nights and an odd weekend. But drag the special project out for more than a month and he is going to start asking questions.

TIP Be as nonspecific as possible. Don't nail down a time and place. Lies of omission harder to track.

RULE 2: GET A BACK-UP BUDDY.

You need someone who will swear to the lies you are telling, affirm you are going out with them when you are really out with your bit on the side and give the heads-up signal if they note that your boyfriend is getting suspicious.

TIP Since almost everyone in the world – no matter how close to you – is going to tell all sooner or later, your best bet is to choose someone you have something on so you have leverage and can buy yourself more time.

RULE 3: DO NOT PULL A DOUBLE WHAMMY.

Never forget the basic rules of what friends do and don't do. Let's take a second to think about this. Should I sleep with someone that nobody knows or my guy's best friend since school? Hmm, that's a tough one.

RULE 4: KEEP YOURSELF CLEAN.

Perfume or cologne should disguise any smell, but don't overdo it. Also check for stray hairs on your clothes.

TIP **Carry an extra set of underwear.**

RULE 5: USE PROTECTION.

Your cheating ways are putting your partner at risk of STIs/STDs. It's the very least you can do.

Four ways to catch a cheat

Is he working a Free Market behind your back? The best sign that your man is sleeping around is spotting a naked woman bouncing up and down on top of him. But most clues are likely to be subtler.

1. Check his body language.

The day he starts wearing clothes that he previously put on only if you were going somewhere special on a Saturday night, there's usually another woman. If he's also reluctant to kiss you or have sex with you, there's a good chance he's getting it somewhere else.

2. Watch him.

If he's leading a double life, he'll avoid making plans. And his habits will change. If he is a workaholic and suddenly he's leaving work early to 'go out for a drink with the guys', beware. Same applies if he begins self-improving or goes jogging a lot (especially if his clothes never seem sweaty).

3. Get proof.

Unless he wants to get caught (and push you to break up with him), he won't leave dumb clues like a lipstick-stained collar. But he's likely to be unaware of certain other signals a woman can leave on him. Check his clothes out for the smell of her perfume (or worse).

4. Confront him.

If you are almost-but-not-quite 100 per cent sure, tell him you've noticed a change in him lately and you're worried that he's interested in someone else. It's unlikely he'll 'fess up but he *will* head straight for the nearest phone to consult with his amour. In which case, you can really confront him with an 'Aha!' (then get ready to spend the rest of the night discussing your relationship – or the end of it).

True confessions

How much do you reveal about your indiscretion?

You didn't get caught; now you are racked by guilt.
Telling will only make you feel better. And even then, it's a lot like giving in to that craving for a super-sized chocolate bar. You feel good – but temporarily. Then you feel worse – not because of anything you are doing but because he is now questioning your every move, treating you like a suspect about to commit another crime. Do you really need this? Your goal in a relationship is long-term survival, not deprogramming sessions every day.

You cheated and you know it wasn't a one-off.

One-offs are the result of, say, a long-distance relationship, last-minute longings or springtime horniness. Tell him. Then put both of you out of your misery and break up with him.

He caught you.

Keep your cool if confronted on your cheating ways. Maintaining a calm and patient manner will quickly resolve any pressing questions your boyfriend throws at you.

Nine all-purpose excuses for cheating

1. It sort of happened.
2. I was really drunk.
3. You were so sure I had cheated I felt I might as well go ahead and do it.
4. He reminded me so much of you (I bet you'd really like him).
5. I wanted to find out if I really love you or not, and the good news is I do.
6. You were gone for a whole day and I was very, very lonely.
7. Remember how you said you wish I were more spontaneous?
8. He was an ex and I left him for you.
9. Now we're even (even if he didn't cheat, he may think he has treated you so heinously in some other way that he deserved to be cheated on, and if he did cheat and you didn't know about it, well then...).

TIP Never believe a man who has cheated on his girlfriend with you.

Revenge

That rat bastard made you suffer – now it's your turn to make him twist in the wind. Retaliation in general is risky so think it over before you lash out. For example, here's just one way it could boomerang and hit you right in the head: you send him a picture of you having steamy sex with another man. So he sends it on to your mother. Ouch.

Still sometimes a girl's gotta do what a girl's gotta do. So exercise damage control. No sex with him or his best friend as revenge – it will backfire on you since sex is hormonal and emotional.

There are better ways to settle the score.

- Send him pizza every day **at 3 am** – you lost sleep on his account, he might as well lose sleep on yours.
- If you still have the keys to his apartment, sneak in and **hide all his remotes** – he made you feel out of control, now you're returning the favour.
- **Cancel his electricity**, phone and satellite services – if he always kept you in the dark about his secret life, you're going to put out his lights (metaphorically speaking).

In other words, make the punishment fit the crime.
And keep it simple. Otherwise you may end up having your say in court… as defendant. So no physical pain (assault, battery and intent to harm), entering his apartment without access because you know he never locks his bedroom window (breaking and entering), and/or no threats (harassment).

TIP Living well really is the best revenge.

IS HONESTY THE BEST POLICY?

It seems to have become unnecessarily necessary to volunteer all you know, feel and think about everything from your sexual and psychiatric history to intimate assessments of mutual friends – on your first date. This means the second date (if there is one after that emotional spill-all) is spent addressing your and his anxieties about those confessions: 'No, it wasn't really herpes – it was a misdiagnose.' 'I didn't mean to suggest you have to come with me to my Sex Addiction meetings.' 'No, I've never been to an orgy – I just wondered what they were like.' Yes, some things he needs to know but here's how to avoid the 'foot-in-mouth' syndrome.

WHAT TO KEEP YOUR MOUTH FIRMLY SHUT ABOUT (even under penalty of torture or promise of a trip to a secluded Caribbean island)

- **Personal sex history.**
  Okay, so you once worked as a lap dancer, slept with half your graduating class, had an affair with your old boss or have a recurring fantasy about Britney Spears (especially the fantasy). It will only cause him unnecessary worry.

- **How many people you have slept with.**
  Forget all the equations you've heard, like divide your number by three then subtract two, and so on. Save yourself the arithmetic because any number is too high, and he doesn't actually want to know. Yes, his penis will want a woman who knows what she is doing. But his brain – primitive object that it is – will start obsessing about your past lovers ('Is my penis as big? Will it stay as hard?'). He wants you to use every trick you ever learned but spare him the details of how you learned them.

- **You once cheated on a boyfriend with his friend.**
  Never spill. And place a gag on all witnesses. Swear the ex's best friend to secrecy on pain of death or removal of his penis, whichever is easiest.

- **You had a nose job or other cosmetic surgery.**
  Not knowing will not hurt your relationship in any way and will ensure damage control should you ever break up.

- **You've been pregnant and had an abortion.**
  This has nothing to do with him.

TIP You don't even have to tell the person you got pregnant with. Yes, it is a nice courtesy and he may want to be there for you. But what if this is someone you don't see a future with at all? Since it is your future that is going to be in jeopardy, not his, then you should do what you need to do and not worry about him. If you tell him, he may want to weigh in on your decision or even insist you keep the child. If you have regrets, visit him six months after – you'll see in the cold, clear light of day that you made the right decision.

...AND WHAT'S OKAY TO SPILL RIGHT AWAY

- **Lies you told to pick him up.**
  You are a computer analyst and now you need help with your computer)

  - **You see a shrink and/or take antidepressants.**
    Neither are that much of a stigma these days and antidepressants may make sex difficult for you (something he will want to know so he can stop blaming himself). If it turns him off, then something is wrong with him.

- **Your current relationship status.**
  If you are in the middle of breaking up with someone, let him know so he understands your mood changes.

WHAT YOU SHOULD KEEP QUIET ABOUT UNTIL IT'S CLEAR YOU ARE GOING TO GET HORIZONTAL

- **Your sexual health history.**
  Unsafe sex, especially with a practising bisexual/needle-sharing IV drug user/recipient of untested blood) all fall into the Need To Know category, along with currently infectious STIs/STDs.

  - **Preferred birth control.**
    It's best you concur before you get naked or he may assume you are on The Pill while you assume that he is packing a coat for his penis.

- **Whether anal lovemaking is a personal favourite.**
  This is considered high-risk sex and he has a right to know if it is a regular habit of yours.

...AND HE IS ABOUT TO PUT A RING ON YOUR FINGER

- **You have a family history of mental illness or substance abuse.**
  Lay your genetic cards on the table only if you're serious enough to talk babies.

  - **You're a rape or sexual-abuse survivor.**
    If you tell too soon he may worry or see you as damaged.

- **You have a criminal record.**
  If you are going to share credit cards, a bank account and/or a mortgage.

  - **You have had a relationship with another woman.**
    If it was a fun romp, no. But if she was the love of your life you will eventually need to talk about it.

Will he talk?

The more yes answers you give, the more likely he is to talk behind your back.

- Is he a big talker? If he is, he's capable of motor-mouthing your secrets – they make too good a story not to tell.

- Has he told you about sex with all of his exes – would you rather have not known?

- Does he spill the intimate details of his friends (such as, this one abuses prescribed drugs, that one has trouble getting it up)?

- Do his best friends seem to know everything about him?

TIP Even if he is not into macho one-upmanship, he may start to sing should he ever go solo. Especially if he is the injured party.

What should you never say to a man?

(Unless you want to make him feel like you've fed his penis to the dogs.)

- **Tease him** about his hair, love handles, height or manhood.
  (You'll get as good as you're giving).
- Ask any of the following: '**Do you love me?**', 'Was I
  good?' 'How good was I?' 'Was I better than your last
  lover?' (Think – do you really want him to answer honestly?)
- 'What are you **thinking about**?' (Usually it's a great match
  or if there's any chance of getting your best friend – or any
  woman he's met in the last month – into bed.)
- **Baby talk** in bed. (Are you practising for the real thing?)
- 'But whipped **cream is fattening**.' (This one doesn't really
  need an explanation, does it?)

What he should never say to you (too soon)

'Commitment.' Why do men assume they are so desirable that every woman
wants to spend the rest of her life – or at least her good years – with him?

Hold the action

Your sex life should only be embarrassing because it's so good you don't want
to tell your friends for fear you'll make them feel bad about their own pitiful
manoeuvrings. But occasionally you can get immersed with a man or a sex
act that you simply can't share with your girl posse – because you don't want
to receive the 'YOU DID WHAT?' stare.

Seven **dating situations** it's better to zip up about

1. Dating Down
2. He lives with his parents
3. The ex you made your friends trash for two weeks
4. A girlfriend's ex
5. He's so ugly he's sort of sexy – well, to you anyway
6. That dork (with the most enormous penis)
7. He has HIV

And seven **sex moves** you never want to admit to

1. Sex with no protection
2. Golden showers
3. If your lover falls asleep in the middle of doing it with you
4. Gay man sex
5. Ugly lesbian sex
6. No orgasm sex on a regular basis
7. Sex that involves no touching of the clitoris

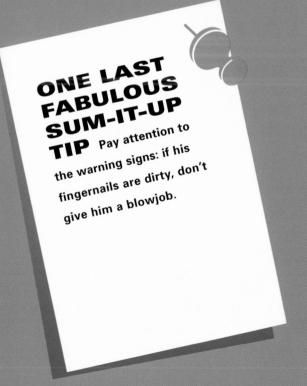

ONE LAST FABULOUS SUM-IT-UP TIP Pay attention to the warning signs: if his fingernails are dirty, don't give him a blowjob.

CHAPTER SEVEN
GETTING PROTECTED

OR 'THERE IS A POINT IN EVERY WOMAN'S LIFE WHEN SHE SAYS "SHOULDA, COULDA, WOULDA..."'

What is a **man's idea** of safe sex?
A padded headboard.

BE AS PICKY ABOUT BIRTH CONTROL AS YOU ARE ABOUT CHOOSING LOVERS. ABSTAINING NEVER BRINGS HAPPINESS SO USE THIS CHAPTER TO FIND THE PROTECTION THAT WORKS FOR YOU.

HOW NOT TO GET PREGNANT
What to wear to bed tonight

IF YOU... USE	MALE CONDOM	FEMALE CONDOM	IUD/IUS
Hate getting stuck in routines	✳ (endless varieties and you can vary how you put them on)		✳
Are in the middle of a dry spell	✳	✳	
Are on a Trampage (or think he is)	✳	✳	
Are in a long-distance relationship	✳	✳	
Think of him as a Male Slut, Fuck Buddy or Freelancer or suspect him of using the Free Market	✳	✳	
A Doucher (or he is)	✳		
Smoke and/or have a family history of heart disease or high blood pressure	✳	✳	✳
Are or are with someone who is Trysexual or Ambisextrous	✳	✳	
Are overweight	✳	✳	✳
Never want a baby			
Will freak if you get an STI/STD	✳ (not 100% safe)	✳ (not 100% safe)	
Can't stop once you start			✳

ORAL CONTRACEPTION	DIAPHRAGM/CAP	HORMONAL IMPLANT/INJECTION	SPERMICIDE	STERILIZATION
		✳		✳
	✳		✳	
	✳			
	✳	✳	✳	✳
		✳	✳	✳
				✳
✳	✳	✳		✳

USE	MALE CONDOM	FEMALE CONDOM	IUD/IUS
Want to be ready for sex at the drop of your pants		✳	✳
Often have one-nighters	✳	✳	
Are taking advantage of Free Market sex	✳	✳	
Hate hassle			✳
Are sleeping with someone who has an STI/STD	✳ (not 100 per cent failsafe against some infections)	✳	
Have an STI/STD	✳	✳ (not 100 percent failsafe)	
Are an Anal Assailant (or he is)	✳	✳	
Are forgetful	✳	✳	✳
Are going to have Leftover Sex	✳ (you don't know where it's been since you last played with it)	✳	
Like high-impact sex	✳ (if combined with pill or spermicide)	✳	✳
Don't want to take hormones	✳	✳	✳ (IUD users only)
Want to reduce the mess during period sex		✳	
Tend to dry out	✳ (if it comes with its own lube)		
Like him to stay inside you after		✳	✳

ORAL CONTRACEPTION	DIAPHRAGM/ CAP	HORMONAL IMPLANT/ INJECTION	SPERMICIDE	STERILIZATION	
✸	✸	✸	✸	✸	
		✸		✸	
				✸	
✸		✸	✸	✸	
	✸		✸	✸	
	✸ (diaphragm users only)				
	✸		✸		
✸	✸	✸	✸	✸	

Don't **screw up** when you **screw around**

Twenty common **birth-control blunders** and how to bust them.

Oral contraceptives

- You **forgot to swallow** your pill: if you do skip one, take two the next day and use added protection – like a condom – for the rest of the month. Don't worry if you experience a little spotting – it's simply your body's way of adjusting to the lower level of hormones.

- Your **prescription ran out**: ask your doctor for a refillable prescription and get it rebooted BEFORE the end of your current pack. AND keep another pack so you won't ever be left high and dry. The leftover pills can serve as 'insurance' doses for up to a year.

- You're on **antibiotics**: ask the chemist if they reduce the effectiveness of your oral contraceptives.

- You **puke** within two hours of taking a pill, have severe diarrhoea or a temperature of 39.4°C (103°F) or above: use something else because your pill may not work.

- You use **St John's Wort**: a commonly used remedy for depression and mood disorders, the herb may interfere with the hormones in contraceptive pills, blocking their efficacy.

Spermicide

- You had sex immediately after applying the stuff: next time, wait an hour for the spermicide to take effect.

IUD

- Losing the string: you need to check for the string extending from your cervix monthly. If you can't feel it, use alternative contraception and call your doctor.

Diaphragm/Cap

- It slipped: make sure you know where your cervix is and that it's fully covered.
  - Removing it too soon: both forms of contraception need to **stay in place** for six hours after sex.
  - Forgetting to use more spermicide if you have sex again or three hours or more after inserting your diaphragm/cap: next time, keep a tube ready for easy application.
- You **want it wetter**: don't use petroleum products – jelly, baby oil or lotion – if your shield is made of rubber, they'll eat a hole right through. Instead, stick with water-based love grease.
- It's stuck: **vigorous sex** can sometimes shove a diaphragm way up a vagina where it's difficult to reach. If this happens, get into a squatting position and bear down with your abdominal and pelvic muscles. This will force the shield downward to a point where it's accessible. Try to relax or you'll make your muscles more tense. If the contraceptive hasn't budged for 24 hours, get to the doctor or you risk infection.
  - You gained or lost weight: have your diaphragm refitted after each vaginal birth or 4.5 kg (10 lb) **weight change**.
  - Maintenance: once a month, check for small holes. Take it when you have your yearly pelvic, so your doctor can check the fit. Replace it every 12 to 18 months or any time it becomes stiff, grungy or discoloured.

Male condoms

- It slipped off: use a condom made to fit snugly.
- It broke: next time, **leave some space** at the end if the condom isn't made to take the force of his shooting.
  - It tore: don't open the packet with a nail file, scissors or teeth.
  - It gives your vagina carpet burn: use one that comes with lubrication. If your condom is rubber, don't use any oil-based lubrication as that will destroy it.

Female condom

- **It slipped**: next time, push the ring up past the pubic bone. Make sure the outer ring and part of the sheath are outside your vagina over the vulva.

Hormonal implants/injections

- You forgot your tri-monthly shot: if you had **sex post-shot** date, you'll need to get a blood test to make sure you're not pregnant. If you aren't, you can get your injection right away. But you should use condoms as a backup for the next two weeks.

OOPS!

The condom broke. The diaphragm slipped. You got taken away by the moment. You don't need to buy a baby name book just yet. You have two choices and a (little) bit of time when your contraception crashes.

1. Emergency Contraception (EC) – aka the 'morning after pill'. These high-dose birth control pills will usually prevent a pregnancy.

However, they MUST be taken within 72 hours of unprotected sex (followed by a second dose 12 hours later), so you can't 'wait and see what happens'.

2. An IUD – this must be fitted within five days of unprotected sex.

TIP ECs don't prevent infection. Washing your vagina with mild soap and water may help. But DON'T douche – it increases the risk of pelvic inflammation and can push sperm in deeper.

LOVE GLOVE

Suits you, sir

You should always offer help with **the condom**. Admittedly, there's not much you can do, but would you show up at a dinner party and not offer to help the hostess?

No man past the knuckle-dragging stage of evolution will take offence at being asked to wear a condom. It's just that some moments are better than others. For instance, 'Mmm, oh, God... do you have a, oh, that's good, maybe we should stop and – oh! – you really have to, aaah, right there, uh-huh, let me get a, ooh, higher, that's it, ooohh – WAITAMINUTE! GET THAT THING OUT OF ME! I'VE TOLD YOU FOUR TIMES TO USE A RUBBER!' is not the best time.

Generally, first penis sighting is a good cue that it's time to speak up. After that, the pace is going to pick up. The best approach is a pleasant, yet direct, statement like 'We have to use a condom'. It leaves no room for misinterpretation or negotiation. But there are other ways to help him accessorize.

- **When he's fully standing to attention, nibble on his ear and whisper, 'Let me put a condom on you.'**
  To do it with finesse, gently squeeze the tip to get rid of air. This will also help you roll the condom on the right way round. Put a drop of lubricant on his penis (water-based only as anything made of oil can rot the condom). Still holding the tip, roll the condom all the way down the penis (if it won't go to the base then it's probably on inside out).

TIP If he is uncircumcised, push the foreskin back while you're putting the condom on. Once most of his penis is covered, you can push the foreskin up again gently.

- **Dominate him.**

  Tell him to roll over, grab a condom, tear the packet open (remembering to avoid sharp objects) and put it on him on one swift motion.

TIP Keep condoms to hand so there won't be a lapse in momentum. Recommended stash points: under the bed, beneath the mattress, in a nightstand drawer, in your pocket or bag. Take them out one at a time. Stacking a pile by the nightstand will put too much pressure on him.

- **Tell him he'll last longer**.

- **Put it on with your mouth.**

  The choice of condom is of major importance. Taste rules. Those doused with spermicide are positively gagging. The best are unlubricated and mint flavoured. Before you begin, make sure your mouth is very, very wet. Remove any tongue, mouth or nose piercings to avoid punctures (in the condom, not his penis). And, to keep the momentum going, open the condom packet now.

  1. He needs to be fairly stiff before you start, so take him in your hands and give him a **firm shake**, if necessary. Once he has a little backbone, hold the condom so the nipple or reservoir at the tip hangs down.

  2. **Suck the nipple** into your mouth, anchoring it against the roof of your mouth with the tip of your tongue (if your condom doesn't have a nipple, flatten about 1 cm (½ in) of the condom with your tongue instead). This is important because if any air gets into the condom, you're going to have a major semen spillage on your hands.

3. Position the rest of the condom **in your mouth** so that the flat circle rests against your front teeth. The nipple should remain firmly against the roof of your mouth until you begin pushing the condom down his member.

4. Now, **gently grasping** his penis shaft with one hand and the thumb and forefinger of the other so only the head and 2.5 cm (1 in) or so below peek through, place your mouth over the head.

5. Immediately slide your lips behind the ring of the condom and push downward so you're gradually pressing the condom down the length of his shaft. If this feels uncomfortable, you can use your hands to slip the condom down to the penis base instead.

- **Offer him a choice** from your Box of Treats (see page 298).

- Hand one over in the **middle of a blowjob** (at this point, there isn't much he won't agree to).
- Smile sweetly and hand him a pre-printed card with a condom taped to it reading, 'You must come dressed for dessert.'

Ouch!

Rolling the condom off a penis can pluck some stray pubic hairs. To prevent this, try to remove the condom like a glove. Some guys like to splash a little cold(ish) water on their penis to encourage shrinkage so the condom can be more easily removed.

Road tests

For:	Buy:
Men who have much to boast about	A condom for larger-sized goods
Mini-mes	Slim-fit condoms for a fit like a glove
A rub-down	A condom with ridges, bumps or extra headroom to give you a bumpy ride
Extra juice	A pre-lubricated glove
Slowing him down	One of the condoms containing 'numbing' lubricant
Mr Softies	A condom with ribs on the inside
That *au natural* feeling	A polyurethane condom (the next-best-thing to skin) – these covers can also be used with oil-based lubricants

Five reasons why a male condom should be a girl's best friend

1. Used correctly, a condom is 98 per cent effective in blocking his sperm and gives you 97 per cent protection against STIs/STDs (see chart opposite). Not bad for something that looks like a reject from a children's birthday party.
2. Condoms slow down Speed Shooters.
3. If you're a Doucher, condoms make sex less messy.
4. You can get one at practically any hour of the day.
5. Many are lubricated, so you don't have to be.

The **highs** and **lows** in the life of a **female condom**

UP	DOWN
It can be put in position up to eight hours before playtime.	You have to remove it immediately after sex.
Used correctly, it's 95 per cent effective against pregnancy and gives you 97 per cent protection from STIs/STDs (except genital warts, herpes and crabs).	The outer ring can slip inside you during sex, reducing effectiveness.
It's made from polyurethane, which is proven to be stronger, thinner and warmer than rubber.	It looks like an upside-down sock. Once inside you, it looks like your guts are hanging out. And (joy of joys) it may squeak.
You can use any type of lubricant, including the oily ones.	You'll need lubricant with your vagina fully clothed in polyurethane.
You don't have to worry about having the awkward 'condom talk' with him.	Putting it on is a lot of hassle for something that can be used only once.

TIP You can stop those late-night condom re-stocking missions after you've been totally true to each other for six months and you've both been tested. AIDS remains extremely rare among women who don't use intravenous drugs and whose partners are heterosexual, drug-free men, but you don't know what he and his favourite muscle have been up to, so it's better to be safe than sorry. For information on testing, see page 249.

PILL POPPERS

The combined pill
This is the Big Mama. It contains two hormones – oestrogen and progestogen.

The pluses and minuses
- It **doesn't interfere** with sex BUT It can give you headaches at first (leading to 'Not tonight, dear…').
- It's **99 per cent effective** against pregnancy BUT it's 0 per cent effective against STIs/STDs.
- It protects against two **types of cancer** (ovary and womb) BUT you may gain weight when you first start taking it.
- It protects against some **pelvic infections** BUT it can increase your blood pressure.
- It reduces the **risk of fibroids** (noncancerous tumours in the womb), ovarian cysts and some breast disease.

Which one for you?
If you are a Type A personality (slightly obsessive-compulsive? who me?), take the monophasic or 21-day pill. You take one pill a day for 21 days and then no pills for the next seven days. Each pill has the same combination of hormones in it.

If you are good with colours, take the phasic pill. You have two or three sections of different coloured pills in the pack. They contain different amounts of hormone so you must take them in the right order. You take one pill a day for 21 days and then no pills for the next seven days.

If you can barely remember your own e-mail address, take the every-day pill. You take one pill a day for 28 days with no break between packets. There are 21 active pills and seven inactive pills (that don't contain any hormones). You must take these pills in the right order.

TIP Having sex during the seven-day period is only safe if you start the next pack on time. Never start your next pack late or miss any of the first seven pills in the pack. This is much more risky than missing pills in the middle of the pack because during the seven-day break your ovaries are not getting any effects from the pill. And if you take a week-plus break, your ovaries may pop an egg.

The mini pill

This is not the combined pill's cuter younger sister. The mini pill has just one hormone – progestogen, so it is also known as the progestogen-only pill, or POP. It is 98 per cent effective against pregnancy. This pill is for anyone stuck in a rut and happy about it – you must take it at roughly the same time every day (even when you have your period) and there are no breaks between packs of pills. If you're more than three hours late, you can become pregnant.

POP stops pregnancy two ways:
1. By thickening the secretions around the neck of your womb (making it tough for his sperm to craw through).
2. By thinning out the lining to your womb, making it a less-than-ideal breeding ground for your eggs. It may sometimes even stop you from releasing an egg.

Bonus 1 You take your first POP on the first day of your period and are immediately protected against pregnancy (other pills usually take a few weeks to kick in).

Bonus 2 You may save on tampons. Your periods may stop altogether or be irregular, light, or more frequent while taking the POP.

WARTS AND ALL

All it takes is one horizontal mamba of Terror Sex with someone who is infected to get a sexually-transmitted infection (STI), also known as a sexually-transmitted disease (STD). Women and men under age 25 and anyone who has had more than one lover – or whose lovers have had other playmates – are in the high-risk category. Go calculate!

Proceed at your own risk

At least 25 different infections are known to be passed from person to person during sex. So be a Spill Master and don't get naked until you read this.

Unprotected penis in vagina or bottom

You risk:

- Chlamydia
- Genital warts
- Gonorrhoea
- Hepatitis B
- Herpes simplex
- HIV (leading to AIDS)
- Pelvic inflammatory disease (PID)
- Pubic lice
- Scabies
- Syphilis
- Trichomoniasis
- Vaginosis

Unprotected blowjobs or mouth sex

You risk:

- Genital warts
- Gonorrhoea
- Hepatitis B
- Herpes simplex
- HIV
- Syphilis

Unprotected M&Ming

You risk:

- Genital warts
- Herpes simplex
- Pubic lice
- Scabies
- Vaginosis

The best defence against most STIs/STDs and other infections is a rubber or polyurethane condom. However, even a love glove can't always protect you from herpes simplex, genital warts or hepatitis B. The break-out, warts or virus might be in an area that the condom doesn't cover.

You could have an **infection** right **now** and not know it

Many STIs have no **obvious symptoms**. If left untreated, some of these diseases can lead to infertility, cervical cancer, even death. Here are some common signs of infection and their possible causes.

Discharge that is
- chunky or very heavy, with small curds like cottage cheese
- watery
- smelly and/or
- greyish, greenish, yellow or pinkish

...might be due to gonorrhoea, trichomoniasis, chlamydia, vaginosis or candidiasis.

When you have sex or pee, you experience
- itching
- burning
- pain
- general discomfort

...might be chlamydia, gonorrhoea, trichomoniasis, urinary tract infection (UTI) or vaginosis.

Itchy or leaking bum
...might be gonorrhoea.

Tummy ache
...might be chlamydia, gonorrhoea, PID or a UTI.

Pain or bleeding during or after sex and/or between periods

…might be chlamydia or trichomoniasis.

Your period is irregular

…might be gonorrhoea.

You pee a lot more than usual and it hurts

…might be gonorrhoea or a UTI.

You have one or more of these 'down there'

- itching
- rashes
- lumps
- blisters
- sores

…might be herpes simplex, genital warts (especially if you see flat, smooth, small bumps or larger cauliflower-like lumps), syphilis (you notice one or more painless sores or warts lasting around three to four weeks), trichomoniasis (your vagina is itching like crazy and very sore), scabies (you have an itchy rash all around all those folds you never like to look at on your body and there are tiny spots inside the creases), pubic lice (you have itchy skin and a black powder – sans fashion sparkles – appears in your pants) or chlamydia.

You have

- fevers
- headaches
- side/tummy aches
- vomiting sessions
- no appetite
- extreme fatigue – like you have the flu only a lot worse
- night sweats
- swollen glands or a sore throat
- backaches

...might be herpes simplex, HIV , hepatitis B or PID.

Your skin and eyes turn yellow and your pee turns brownish

...might be hepatitis B.

If you experience any of these symptoms after having unprotected sex, see your doctor or a genito-urinary medicine (GUM)/sexual health clinic immediately. Left untreated, they can be painful and uncomfortable or at worst cause permanent damage to your health and your fertility.

Most STIs/STDs can be completely cured with a course of antibiotics or special shampoos/creams if found early enough.

There are exceptions

- **HIV** can be controlled with drugs to slow down the damage done to the immune system.
- **Genital warts** can be controlled with a chemical lotion or cream, by freezing them off or by removing them by laser or surgery.
- **Herpes simplex** can be controlled to a certain extent with prescribed antiviral drugs which may make the sores come back less often and shorten the time they're around when they do return.
- **Hepatitis B** there is a vaccine to prevent infection altogether, but once you are infected there's no cure (although certain drugs can lessen the symptoms).

ALERT The nitrate creams used to cure candidiasis can destroy condoms, rendering them ineffective.

Does he have a **toxic** penis?

If he has **any** of the following, head immediately for the door.

- White, green or yellow discharge or pus
- An extremely red and sore-looking tip or balls that hurt
- Bumps, lumps, blisters, sores or itching
- Pain when urinating, and having to go more often than usual
- Little white balls that look like lint in the hair

ALERT You two have been playing hide the salami with abandon and suddenly he won't let you see or touch his penis. He probably has an STI and is hoping his symptoms will go away rather than dealing with it. But even if the symptoms disappear, he'll still have an STI, and he'll still be able to pass it to you.

1. When he's least expecting it, ask him, **'Do you have a sexually transmitted infection?'** Catch him off-guard and he may be too stunned to lie or to lie convincingly.
2. Make him **show you his cock**, and, even if there aren't visible sores or discharge, get him to see a doctor.

Dirty dick warning!

If he's uncircumcised and he has white smelly stuff resembling cottage cheese under the foreskin, it's smegma (see page 93). He should turn back the skin and clean the area daily. That moist dark environment is a bacteria haven and he could develop a painful infection (and pass it on to you), adhesions or swelling.

Spreading the news

Herpes, genital warts, gonorrhoea, syphilis, AIDS: **not the most fun** topics to discuss with anyone, let alone someone you find drop dead sexy. But this isn't the time to be demure. Here's how to let him know you have an STI/STD.

OLD LOVERS

If you know you **weren't infected** by your current beau, the ethical thing to do is to call all your most recent old lovers and fill them on your new health status. Not so much because you care about whether they are suffering, but because one of them may be a carrier and spreading his bug around. It's up to you whether you want to save womankind or not.

PLOY You don't have to be tactful. If you have his number, phone or, better yet, e-mail, just let him know the deal and then disconnect the conversation ASAP. That is, unless you are in the mood for a who-gave-who-and-who's-to-blame-and-were-you-sleeping-around-and-by-the-way-I-never-could-stand-the-way-you-laugh trip down memory lane.

TIP Depending on where you go to get tested, you may be able to pass this job on to public-health workers whose job it is to trace sex partners of people infected with STIs.

NEW LOVER

This one is harder. You don't want to scare him off.

PLOY He will be less likely to want to run for the hills once he's naked, prone and primed for action. So wait until he's managed to get his tongue beneath the edge of your pants,and then give him The Touch – just a hand on his shoulder that let's him know you have something to say. Look him in the eye and say, 'I come with a few added surprises.' Pause for effect. Then continue, 'Are you familiar with… (name of your STI/STD here – using the clinical term will sound less scary)?' Give him the facts concisely and then tell him how you're controlling it, the general state of your health and how you are going to make sex safe for him. The reality is that most STIs are, hysteria aside, a relatively minor problem in the lives of the vast majority of people who 'suffer' from them.

TIP You absolutely can't tell him? Then you must use a condom and, if you have genital warts or herpes, you can not have sex during an outbreak.

Test yourself

STI/STD testing includes a few simple tests that can be done in your doctor's office or at a clinic. The doctor or clinician will want to know your sexual history (be honest – they've heard it all) and any symptoms you're experiencing. Depending on what you are being tested for, you'll get the results in any time from an hour to one week.

The physical exam

First they'll check out your genitals for sores or lesions. Then they'll do a pelvic exam and take a smear or swab test to get a small sample of cells and fluids. They may also take a sample of cells from your throat and/or rectum. You may be asked for a saliva sample, urine sample, blood sample or any combination of these. A blood test is the most common way to test for HIV and syphilis.

Pussy posse

It's no fun dealing solo with the worry over what the result of the test will be. So turn the ordeal into a gal-pal support party.

1. Gather ten of your closest girlfriends.
2. Put out bowls of different types of condoms.
3. Plaster walls with ***Playgirl* pictorials** of naked men.
4. Mix a pitcher of Cosmopolitans or your favourite drink.
5. Talk about good **places to meet guys** if you have an STI/STD (such as at the clinic – a good opening line is matching your infection).
6. Discuss the pros and cons of sex with strangers versus strange sex – cyesolagnia (pregnant women), nanophilia (short people) and melissophilia (insects).
7. Have a session of **kiss and tells** – the most famous person you've slept with and his dirty little secrets.
8. **Dirty dance** to bad 1970s disco music.

ONE LAST FABULOUS SUM-IT-UP TIP The well-dressed girl is always the life of the party. Know how to accessorize and you'll never feel over-packed or unprepared for an overnight trip.

CHAPTER EIGHT

TROUBLES IN PARADISE OR 'YOU KNOW IT'S NOT WORKING WHEN HIS DOG WANTS TO HAVE SEX WITH YOU BEFORE HE DOES'

When is **premature ejaculation** a problem?

When it happens between 'Hello' and 'What's your name?'

BAD SEX. UNFULFILLED SEX. SEX REQUIRING LOTS OF EFFORT AND NOTHING TO SHOW FOR IT. SEX YOU JUST DON'T WANT TO THINK ABOUT. BUT WHATEVER YOUR BEDROOM BLUES, THERE'S AN ANTIDOTE.

BORN-AGAIN VIRGIN

One week turns into two which turns into three which turns into… it's so long since you had any that you get excited about a tampon. Don't go shopping for a black and white wimple quite yet. Your sex life is about to change – tonight. Here's how to conquer born-again-virgin frustration and get your groove back.

Five ways to drench your dry spell

Maybe you haven't had sex in weeks, or maybe when you have it, it's uninspired. **Or orgasm-free**. For those times when your boyfriend or assorted step-ins won't do, you need back-up. Sex is not a luxury like pricey face cream. It's the thing that ensures you wake up with a smile on your face. It's what keeps wrinkles, bad hair days and PMS cramps at bay. Here are some ways to get back in the saddle.

OPTION 1: Have a new fling.

Frustration = big bold mama. If all you are after is sex, just **proposition a guy**. Unless you are two sheets to the wind (and not even then if he's had a few too), you are not going to get turned down.

TIP Choose someone whom you've seen dance (the more comfortable he is grooving down, the more at ease he will be doing a horizontal dance).

OPTION 2: Call an old fling (a really good-in-bed old fling).

Think of this as **Maintenance Sex**. The bonus is you've done it once, so the second time will be even easier. But be clear that all you are expecting is a repeat performance and not a lifetime or even daytime commitment.

OPTION 3: Prevail upon a male friend.

Pick one whose dating habits **smell of hound**. You want someone who won't kiss-and-tell but neither will he kiss-and-stay. Why? Because if you wanted a relationship with him, it would've happened a long time ago.

OPTION 4: Call your ex.

Leftover Sex is perfect for ending your dry spell. He's been there, done that and knows the lay of the land, so satisfaction is guaranteed. But to avoid going over old ground or risk renewing a bad-for-you partnership, keep it light and call the ones who only wanted you for sex (isn't this his lucky day?).

> **TIP** Calling Rules: phone before midnight. After the witching hour is a sign of desperation – you've apparently tapped out your resources at the local club and couldn't find another option.

OPTION 5: Find an 'Er-hem'.

The rules are simple. You are **not boyfriend and girlfriend**; you are lovers. Repeat: you are not boyfriend and girlfriend; you are go-at-it-like-bunnies-because-there-is-no-one-else-in-your-life-right-now-and-damn-you-really-need-some-and-so-does-he. That's it. Nothing more. Do not fantasize about long Sunday brunches doing the crossword puzzle together, or even necessarily breakfast the next morning. This is sex with a purpose and the purpose is sex.

Signs you'll need sex soon

Check **two** or more and it's time to find a **Fuck Buddy**.

- You know it's been two months, 13 days and four hours (and 33 minutes) since you've had sex (but who's counting?).
- You correlate the length of time you've gone without sex with how much of a loser you are.
- You think good thoughts about your ex.
- Dogs are dry-humping your leg – and you say, 'It's OK. Really.'
- You start stalking eligible mattress partners – like the repair guy.
- You have begun to masturbate five to ten times a day.

Dry spell, Part Two

What's worse than a **sexual drought** when you're single? One when you're in a relationship. There are usually three reasons why your sex life hits a dry patch.

- You always play the same position.
- You know exactly how to stimulate each other.
- His penis is tired of your vagina and shoots off in seconds – or worse, not at all.

The quickest and easiest way to **jolt yourselves** out of a sex recession is to keep each other guessing. Change position, change foreplay order, have a Wake-n-Bake – up the ante so neither of you ever know what's going to hit you.

WINNING PLOY 1: TAKE YOUR SHOW PUBLIC

You're some place where you really can't do anything about it… let loose with the **steamy talk**. You'll not be able to wait to get home and put your fire out.

WINNING PLOY 2: THE SURPRISE GIFT

Cliché, true. But there's nothing like a little unexpected lingerie (a good uni-gift) to make the recipient go out of his/her way to express gratitude (read oral sex). Presto: your sex life is back.

The key thing is **don't put sex on hold**. When you first got together, all it took was a flash of an elbow to make you both want to get naked and do dirty things to each other. Now downloading your Palm Pilot takes precedence. But desire doesn't stick around once it's been dissed. You need to be willing to drop everything and do it as soon as you feel even a nudge from your libido. Stick with that and your sex life won't be a trip down memory lane.

HUNT THE ORGASM

When it comes to coming, different women have very different physical and psychological triggers. Some fortunates can reach oh-holy-Jesus every bit as easily as your average man, in almost any position, with little or no extra help. Most women rely on attention to their inspiration point, so it may take a session of intense tongue or finger action to send them over the brink. And some women can't launch until the sun, the moon, the stars and your comet are properly aligned.

So how to **stop the madness** when your orgasm goes undercover? Climaxes are not something you can make happen (especially killer kinds). You may even find that the more you try, the fewer you have. On the other hand you don't need to be a Zen master and forsake all desire for orgasm in order to attain one. The key is to figure out why your Big O has gone AWOL in the first place.

Not tonight, dear, my vagina has a headache

Your vagina is a **sensitive creature**. It needs to be nurtured, cared for and supported. And when it doesn't feel cherished, it is hardly going to be a top-notch orgasm-producing factory. If you haven't been feeling the same old thrill lately, here are some common ailments which could be the cause.

Depressed vagina

You can't have sex, wear tight clothes or use tampons (you're probably getting depressed just reading that). Known medically as **vulvodynia**, the pain from this condition can be so bad that it feels like hot razor blades are stabbing your vaginal area, making some sufferers suicidal. Untreated or recurring bacterial infections such as yeast infections can cause inflammation, which can lead to vulvodynia. The condition has four distinct symptoms.

- **Painful inflammation** at the entrance to the vagina.
- **Stabbing sensations** that travel down into the glands. create pain that is so bad some sufferers can't sit down.
- **Painful spasms** in the muscles of the pelvic floor.
- For some people, shrinkage of the vaginal tissue due to the **extreme pain**. This means that if anyone tries to insert anything into the vagina, the skin will tear, making sex painful and, in some cases, impossible.

Specialized biofeedback therapy (retraining of the pelvic-floor muscles) is often used to reduce the affected area. A small, tampon-like probe with two metal strips is inserted into the lower part of the vagina and monitored on a TV screen as it **picks up electrical signals** from the muscle tissue. You are taught to tense and relax the muscles. After a few sessions with your doctor, you can do the exercises at home using a portable unit for 20 minutes, twice a day. Medications can be used to reduce discomfort. In severe cases, the painful glands can be removed.

Dry vagina

Yowza! Sex when you're dry is about as delightful as rubbing sandpaper on your vagina. Fortunately, this is often an easy problem to fix. If you don't feel wet enough to do the deed comfortably, then start by simply jacking up the foreplay quotient (shame).

But if you're still bone-dry, the cause of your drought may be something else. All sorts of things can dehydrate your body's natural lubing. Medication (from the 21-day or monophasic birth control pill to antidepressants to some over-the-counter antihistamines), nursing, diet (too much salty food), booze, your menstrual cycle, fatigue and even stress can cause you to be **less juicy**.

The no-fail option is to call in the troops and add a dab of over-the-counter lubricant to your vagina during your love play. If you use any sort of rubber protection, choose a water or silicone-based product as oily ones will burn a hole right through your baby stopper. Bonus: it'll feel squishy-wonderful to him too.

Scared vagina

Double Bed Dread, not being able to live out your **Secret Single Behaviour**, being with someone who is not a Spill Master – these are all reasons your vagina gets freaked. You need to take things slowly and talk with your boyfriend about what's making you lose it.

Another reason a vagina gets scared is if you have been the victim of rape or abuse. If this is your situation, you need a gentle, loving partner and a counsellor or psychotherapist who can help you to feel more secure.

Angry vagina

For some women, **foreplay** is everything that happened in the last 24 hours. Which means if you're ticked off with your partner for any reason, you're going to need to hash it out first... and then have make-up sex.

Bored vagina

You've moved beyond the stage when you **stayed up until 3 am**, bonking six times a night. You've settled into one style of lovemaking to the point where you can even predict within minutes how long your encounters will last and, although you probably alternate between a few favourite positions, the overall effect is the same: routine sex. Which is sure to send your vagina to sleep.

There are three simple ways to keep the passion impulse cranked up to high. Make him constantly:

- **yearn for it...** by jumping his bones in the shower or first thing in the morning – whenever and wherever you don't normally make love.
- **burn for it ...** by telling him at a wildly inconvenient moment (in the middle of a night out at the movies or when you're stuck on the bus) that you're going to give him such a good time later that he's going to leave his body three times and then beg to get back into it when he sees how much fun it's having.
- **learn from it...** by calling him the morning after and telling him exactly what he did to make you really hum and how you're looking forward to him doing it again ASAP).

Stressed vagina

One sure way not to have an orgasm is to **focus hard** on having one. If you're stressed about climaxing, you may have trouble getting aroused because the blood flow to the area is restricted. Then there's the usual daily stress you might be experiencing in your life (your boss wants your project last week, your boyfriend is pressuring you for some kind of commitment, you're having an affair, your goldfish died...). This sort of stuff can stress out your vagina too. And when the stress disappears, your orgasms will reappear. (See also Ouch! That hurts! on page 267.)

Drugged vagina

Drugs, tobacco and alcohol have been shown to make your **orgasm shy**.

Sick vagina

If you've never had an orgasm, you **may need a blood test**. Injuries or abnormal growths on the anterior pituitary gland can prevent you from exploding. Once the lesions are surgically removed, you'll become orgasmic.

Instant orgasm killers

Guys into Goalie sex. Guys who shout obscenities (or worse, some other darling's name) in the middle of sex. It's enough to make your orgasm leave town permanently. But these are small potatoes. Here's what really counts as orgasm-cide.

- His dick smells of pee when you go down on him.
- He takes a dump in front of you.
- He has skid marks in his underwear.
- When he goes down on you, his tongue action is so hard it's like he's trying to knock your clitoris out.
- He leaves wet slug trails when he's licking your body.
- Once he actually locates your clitoris, he doesn't leave it alone.
- Earlingus – there are better places for his tongue.
- He leaves his socks on in bed. (Does he know how ridiculous he looks?)
- He's guilty of the three evils: back hair, navel lint and toe jam.

Ouch! That hurts!

Love hurts. Sex shouldn't. If the pain is coming from deep inside, you may have pelvic inflammatory disease or endometriosis (when some of the tissue that normally lines the uterus is displaced to lie outside it, causing pain when he thrusts). But the cause may also be one of two stress-related conditions.

Pelvic pain syndrome

It seems that chronic stress alters the flow of blood in the veins of the pelvis so that it **becomes congested**. If you are easily aroused during sex, but have difficulty reaching orgasm, the problem becomes worse because the pelvic congestion cannot be relieved by climax (in other words, you've got the female equivalent of blue balls). You may then experience a pain that persists after sex for some hours until the congestion is dispersed.

Vaginismus

You're involuntarily contracting the band of muscles around your vaginal opening when anything tries to poke its head in. The more you're poked, the more you squeeze. Some women shriek when anything is inserted into their vagina – from a slender-sized tampon to a pencil penis. Even a finger can make them squirm (and not with pleasure). The result: **extreme pain**. Treatment is generally relaxation exercises prescribed by a reputable sex therapist.

Pleasing me

Sometimes the best cure for an elusive orgasm is a little self-help. You can generally turn yourself on quicker than anyone else because you know what makes your love organs sing arias and what makes them screech. If hand-to-vagina combat doesn't make you peak, you may need to add some cliterature. Eventually the orgasm genie will appear.

Five Ways to Get His Penis in the Mood

1. Keep the lights on when you get undressed.
2. Purr seductively, 'It's the biggest I've ever seen'.
3. Tickle it's chin – the underneath part where it's ultra-sensitive.
4. Juice it up with plenty of lube (the pre-bought kind or saliva).
5. Give it a ride between your breasts.

FLOPPY DICKS

His dick is under a **lot of pressure**. Think about it. You expect it to snap to attention the second you make eye contact with his jeans – even when the body it's attached to is drunk, sick, or completely lost in the final two minutes of the match. Then you expect it to remain as **hard as Superman's pecs** until you have your total body meltdown. At which time, you expect it to explode with no prolonged handling required.

Unfortunately there is no shortage of things that can go wrong with the penis. And the one thing you can be sure of is that every guy will go limp at some point in his life. Which means today may be your unlucky day.

It doesn't work

Required techniques to tame, train and treat his penis.

Now you see it, now you don't
If you two are always body banging after a night of drinking or a five-star meal, chances are you are going to be playing hide-and-seek with his erection.

TO DO If you want a better night life, it's time to stop living quite so much of the good life.

Putting on a condom can also make him sag mid-action. Hey, would you want to get rubber-suited if it isn't raining out?

TO DO Have some sympathy and keep the atmosphere sexy by massaging his favourite digit as the condom rolls on. That should keep his passive-aggressive penis from fading out.

He's a limp noodle
If this is the first time you've **played together**, first-night jitters may be turning him into a late bloomer. Women aren't the only ones who get self conscious when they get naked for the first time. He knows he's expected to perform like a stud, he wants to perform like a stud, so Murphy's Law says there will be no tools to perform like a stud with.

TO DO Give him a kiss, say there's other things you can do together and chances are he'll find his inner bone.

His compulsion to wilt turns into a regular show

If you've been together for a while, the culprit may be one of the following: major job hassles, he's extremely pissed off at you, he's whacked (as in tired), **he's whacked** (as in wanking too much), or he's freaked (as in, 'I think I'm in love with this woman' or 'I'm engaged to this woman and I have no idea who she is').

TO DO The only way to know for sure is to talk it out. If the problem continues and you've ruled out all the above, he may want to see his doctor. Less common causes are illness, medication or neurological problems.

TIP The quickest way to get a man hard is to go straight to the heart of the matter: his penis. Use a firm grip, a wet hand and flick your tongue. But if you've been working at it a while and he just won't get hard, it's time to stop when your hand goes numb. Then ask him gently to crank himself up – and if that doesn't work, get him to diddle around with your downstairs equipment until he's standing to attention. If that fails, you really are backing a loser.

He won't shoot

Unless he's been hanging out with Sting, chances are the boy has been having a little **too much self love**. The friction a guy gives himself during a meat-pounding session is a lot more intense than anything your vagina can provide.

TO DO First he needs to lay off his five-on-one games. This will put him more in the mood for what you have on offer. Then, doing it doggy should tighten things up (although, frankly, it will never replace the sweetness of his own hand).

He never wants any

This often happens after you **start living together** and he becomes too familiar with the machinery. Or, if you've been the bone jumper, it may be that he's got used to waiting for your signal. Or, if this is how he has always been, he may have a low sex drive. The first two you can fix. The third you're stuck with. But telling him no more nookie until he makes the first move will only up the pressure on him and probably lead to a case of performance shakes.

TO DO 1 Talk with him about how much you love sex – especially with him – and find out if he feels that he is getting enough. It may be that he does want more but you're simply missing his signals.

TO DO 2 When you're up for it, let him 'catch' you masturbating. You can indicate you want him to join you and then explain that you just don't get enough sex to fulfil you – message transmitted, loud and clear.

He's a Speed Shooter

Like most guys, he probably had his first 100 orgasms or so from churning the butter and has become used to moving at the speed of light. Luckily, you can slow him down to real time.

TO DO 1 Try stopping and starting the action intermittently (see pages 80–81).

TO DO 2 You on top or lying side-to-side makes for slower (less stimulating to him) sex.

TO DO 3 Desensitizers, those magical sprays and creams, can turn a minute man into a marathoner. Using a condom will also put the brakes on him – two will bring him to a screeching stop (though he may feel like he's having sex with a wad of cold, chewed gum).

TIP The good news is if he's in his twenties, his refractory period (the time it takes before he can get another erection) is between 10 and 20 minutes – and that's just long enough to reapply your lipstick!

The foreskin excuse

Uncircumcised men who speed shoot often blame their foreskin, while the circumcised fingerpoint the rapid delivery on not lack of a foreskin. The reality: timing has nothing to do with foreskin.

His dick is permanently dead

The words 'impotence' and **'erectile dysfunction'** (ED) can strike fear into the hearts of even the most reasonable men. Most believe they should always want sex, and that they should always be able to provide a hard penis on command for any willing partner. And quite reasonable those expectations are, too. When he can't – not once, not a few times, but every time – it means he has ED. This doesn't signal the end of his sex life (or yours for that matter).

Erections start in the brain, and end up, well, you know where they end up. But there's a lot of space between the brain and the penis (more with some men than others) and many things can happen to prevent erections.

If he gets hard, but then loses it

Chances are his problems are **psychological** (the most common cause is stress). So he needs to concentrate on relieving the pressures in his life before he can hope to build up any pressure in his penis.

If he's not even leaving the starting gate

The problem could be **medical** (and it will tend to worsen gradually). He's going to have to take a trip to the doctor. A whole slew of conditions – damaged **nerves**, blocked arteries, cardiovascular disease, depression, diabetes, kidney and liver diseases – can permanently affect erections, as can certain medications (antihistamines, appetite suppressants and those for blood pressure). Treatment can range from therapy, through hormone replacement (if there's a imbalance), using a little mini pump device that forces blood up into the penis, to surgery.

SCHIZO SEX IS...

...WHEN YOU LOVE HIS PENIS BUT ARE TIRED OF HIM

You're with a guy who doesn't hit you, doesn't make you go to action flicks, isn't a kid-hating, small-animal-killing, all-around heathen. But, for whatever reason, you know you don't want to spend the rest of your life with him. BUT the sex is finger-burning wonderful. In fact, you've never had any like it.

Q: Do you have to **break up** with someone with whom you have hot sex but not so hot everything else?

A: Actually, you don't have to do anything except pay taxes, die and run into your ex on the one day of the year you haven't washed your hair or put on make-up.

There is nothing wrong with going out with someone just for **the passion**. Face it: you can get companionship (the other pillar of a good relationship) from friends. But maybe you're too involved in work right now to have a relationship. Or you're not in the mood for a relationship. And no, you don't have to alert him that this is for the short term. (Did you ever believe a man when he told you that? Or, if you did, didn't it make you fall all the harder?) If and when he wants more, he'll let you know. And then you can let *him* know. Until then, enjoy what he has to offer.

...WHEN YOU LOVE HIM BUT ARE TIRED OF HIS PENIS

You are dating **Mr Well-He-Seems-Wonderful**. He has a steady job with real potential, he takes you to the best places, tells you how beautiful you look, and calls when he said he would. Your friends like him. Your mother *loves* him. Even your cat purrs around him. What a guy – the embodiment of IBM – until you get him home and horizontal.

The only problem is that there are no fireworks. Sex is good – not great, not bad, just okay. You might decide to overlook it, but after a couple of months you recognize little signs that tell you the chemistry is off. His touch annoys you. His scent doesn't turn you on. He's more interested in the sports on TV than getting up to a little wrestling match with you.

While there's nothing wrong with making a few compromises when it comes to love – it's actually a necessity – there is something wrong with making a sacrifice. And while the sex doesn't have to be scrape-you-off-the-ceiling every time, it does need to leave a warm feeling in your belly. You cannot think yourself into sexual attraction. It's either there or it isn't. Here is the **straight truth**: while he may be perfect, he's not perfect for you.

ONE LAST FABULOUS SUM-IT-UP TIP When he says, 'It's not you, it's me,' believe him! When he says, 'I'm a bastard,' believe him! When he says, 'No woman has ever understood me,' believe him! When he says, 'I love you,' and he hands you a ring, believe him!

CHAPTER NINE WILD SEX OR 'IS IT WORTH JOINING A CLUB THAT WANTS YOU AS A MEMBER?'

Is that a **vibrator** in your **pants** or are you just pleased to see me?

YOU MAY NOT BE INTO DRESSING UP LIKE LITTLE BO-PEEP, BUT YOU MIGHT STILL BE TRYSEXUAL ABOUT THE WILD WORLD OF SAFE, CONSENSUAL KINK, INCLUDING PROPS, PORN, GAMES AND GROUPS. HERE'S YOUR GUIDE TO THE EROTIC AND EXOTIC – NO EXPERIENCE NECESSARY.

TOP PLACES TO LAY YOUR BOOTY

Why stay at home when there's a whole wide world out there?

Bar/Restaurant bathroom

You may not want to sit on the toilet seat but you can kneel on it to make **standing sex** easier.

TIP Unless you want to be invaded by a gaggle of women discussing everything from periods to pantyhose and pubic hairs, all while serenaded by a cascade of urine, hold out for a single-occupancy bathroom.

Pool/Beach

What could be more blissful than **frolicking in water**? Since you're almost weightless in water, it's easy to do things you wouldn't normally be able to do. However, since water washes away natural lubrication, it can make thrusting as much fun as using a nail-studded vibrator unless you load up with some non-water-based lubricant first. Your hottest choice is to be in a mutually exclusive relationship since condoms and water don't really mix. Then you can use any old grease and float away to bliss. However, if you are still at the love-glove stage, look for a silicone-based and therefore rubber-condom-compatible one. The perfect water level is waist high (any lower and it's embarrassing, any higher and you may get swept away along with your passion – literally). Once you're slippery, move to chest-deep water and wrap your legs around him.

TIP Hold onto your bikini bottoms. You don't want to do the Walk of Shame back to your towel.

Your friendly neighbourhood hot tub

An alternative to the chlorinated swimming pool or salt water and strange microscopic life. Hot tubs are warm, bubbly, steamy, perfect places to get all **hot and bothered**. Take a seat on the little ledge and go to it while jets of water massage you all over. Or make love sitting face to face while the bubbles wash over you.

TIP Soaking in a hot tub causes shrinkage so his erection may not be all it could be.

Photo booth

Swivel the stool to make your pictures private. The higher you go, the more likely the camera will **catch you in action**.

Restaurant

Make sure the establishment is fancy enough to have **large napkins**. Once you're seated, line his lap with the linen. Then slip your hand under the table and **unzip him**. Give him an appetizing hand-job, using the napkin to mop up any mess. He can reciprocate the favour.

TIP Take the napkin home with you (but don't save it à la Monica Lewinski unless you think he is destined for higher places).

Fitness equipment

Calf-raise machines, hip stretchers, abdominal boards – all lend themselves to several hundred **kinky moves**. Just be sure to wipe the sweat off when you finish your set.

Elevator

You can try the one to your hotel room, but alarms, video security cameras and bellhops make it likely you'll get caught. Instead, use a freight lift. It won't have an alarm and you can stop it **between floors** for more privacy.

Lingerie shop

What's more fun than combining two enjoyable activities in one big shebang? Choose a shop with large fitting rooms that's used to women asking if their men can come in to **approve the wares**. To be undetected, the best idea would be either to cosy up on the changing bench or against the wall (unless you're in a shoddy cubicle which will probably collapse).

TIP Don't stain merchandise that you can't afford to buy.

Tight closet at a boring party

Squeeze in and cuddle up. But make sure **your clothing** is rearranged before rejoining the party. That includes a once over for any spare mittens or scarves that static have left clinging to your back.

Taxi

Give the driver a **far-away destination** so there's plenty of time to have fun. Most taxis have dividers between driver and passenger and if you are discreet about groping each other the driver won't even know what you're up to – unless you want him/her to!

Quick moves

Speed is a key factor in an out-of-house romp – you'll need to make yourself presentable pretty quick if interrupted. So make sure you are dressed for it. No complicated hooks or ties on your trousers, and panties should be manoeuvrable enough to slide to the side when there's no opportunity to take them off. Boxer shorts seem made with quickies in mind: most gape open the moment you put them on.

FREAK YOUR SEX LIFE

Has sex become as predictable as your **morning commute**? Do you long to deviate from your daily routine? Here are a few shortcuts to getting waylaid.

Bottoms up sex

Five things you've gotta love about rear-ending.

1. You don't have to be an Anal Assailant to enjoy the thrill of entering the **forbidden zone** – because it's considered dirty, it automatically becomes hot.
2. It's **two holes** in one (for all you golf buffs).
3. It's just so **much tighter** back there (not that your vagina feels like a train tunnel or anything).
4. It's chock-a-block full of **sexy nerves**, which could mean a stronger orgasm for you.
5. You won't get **pregnant**.

How to knock down the back door

Most women aren't exactly thrilled at the prospect of having something that feels like a 18 x 7.5 cm (7 x 3 in) sausage shoved into an area that only shares gifts with the toilet bowl. Which is why the key for happy ass love is going **s-l-o-w-l-y**.

STEP 1 It's not a vagina; it doesn't secrete fluid. So use **lubricant** – and lots of it – otherwise, you'll jump up to the ceiling and dig your nails into the lighting fixture. The best grease is a silicone water-based lube. They're slick and slidey and stay that way longer.

STEP 2 Work the fingers – **one well-lubed digit** at a time. Once you're comfortable with him easing one finger in, he can slide in another. At first, your rectal muscles may feel tight due to nervousness, but the more anal foreplay he gives you with his fingers, the more they'll relax.

STEP 3 When you're warmed-up and ready for something bigger, apply generous lubrication to his penis or to the condom. Avoid positions where he has control of **thrusting duties**, like doggy-style. Have him lie on his back and hop on top.

STEP 4 Time to ease him in, and you have several options.

- He can **rub his penis** against your opening. This external stimulation should relax the anus. As the sphincter muscles contract, the opening appears to 'wink', which is his signal that it's now time to slide in.
- He can **press his penis** against your opening (you will find that you want to either relax or bear down in order to let him in).
- He can start with his finger, withdraw it, and while your hole is open, gently **insert his penis**.

STEP 5 Take it slow to give **your ass the opportunity** to get used to his penis. He should keep his movements gentle and subtle at first. When you're ready, he can venture further inside and start some slow thrusting. The rectum is not a straight tube. It's shaped more like an 'S'. So when he plunges, he should adjust the angle of his dangle and aim for the belly button. If it starts to hurt after he's advanced a little, he's probably hit the curve. Have him stop and pull back a smidgen to let you adjust. The more you relax, the more your rectum elongates and the curve lessens. After a moment, he can go a little deeper.

▼ FREAK OUT LEVEL IF HE WANTS IT AND YOU DON'T

One Cosmopolitan

It's not like he wasn't interested in exploring your erogenous zones.

On a role

Sexy lingerie is one thing, but getting decked out in full Princess Leia regalia, complete with earmuff hair and R2D2 at your heels may be a bit too far out in space. Decide where you're willing to go with this **trick or treat** – you can rent anything from a nurse's outfit to a Cinderella dress.

▼ FREAK OUT LEVEL IF HE WANTS IT AND YOU DON'T

One Cosmopolitan.

It's good for a laugh with the girls later.

Tie me up, Tie me down

There's nothing like tying up a man to remind a girl that she's in charge of her life.

HOW TO FOOL HIM INTO BEING TIED UP

Not every guy is going to be comfortable with the idea of being put at your mercy when the idea is presented to him on a cold platter, so you need tactics.

• **Be prepared** – if you spend 20 minutes looking for something to tie him up with, it is going to take the excitement out of the proceedings. Skip scratchy twine and scary ropes and opt for skin-friendly materials, like scarves, neckties and fishnets. Slip them under the pillow or out of sight but within easy reach.

• **Once you're both comfortably naked** and more than a little hot and bothered, whisper in his ear that you are going to drive him insane… but he isn't allowed to touch you at all. The more things you do to him, the harder your 'hands off' policy is going to be – and that gives you the opportunity to offer to tie his wrists loosely so you can get on with turning him into a puddle of molten flesh.

DOING THE DEED

Secure his limbs to the bedposts. If you don't have bedposts, you can tie his wrists together. But don't tie his legs together or this will turn into mission impossible. Be careful not to tie too tightly – circulation is a good thing!

Take your time. Slowly lick him and then stop. When you restart, move unexpectedly to another body part. Not knowing what you're going to do next will really drive him wild, to the point where he will be begging you to untie him. And when you do, chances are he returns the favour… and then some.

TIP Using wrist cuffs is much easier than learning to tie knots and safer than using metal handcuffs.

BINDING RULES

1. Decide on a safe word.

You need something you can use when you want or need to come back to reality. **A weird word** that will get the other person to stop and say 'huh?' is usually best. For example, if that strap on your wrist is too tight or that tongue lashing is getting too rough, you say 'Meow'.

2. Buy good equipment.

You don't want the **handcuffs key** to break when one of you is cuffed naked to the bed (for that matter, make sure you keep track of the key).

3. Never let a guy tie you up unless you know him well.

The last thing you want is to 'come to' from **your orgasm** and find him gone and his basset hound licking your feet.

YY FREAK OUT LEVEL IF HE WANTS IT AND YOU DON'T

Two Cosmopolitans

It feels like foreplay under pressure, no matter who gets tied up.

Pain lite

If you want things to get **a little rougher** in bed, wait until you are naked and then whisper, 'I've been a bad girl and I need a spanking' while squirming your bottom over his knees.

RULE 1 To **minimize pain**, the hand should be cupped, distributing the impact more evenly across the bottom.

RULE 2 Best **spanking spot** is the padded area where cheek meets thigh.

RULE 3 Spank close to the **love triangles** and they'll be stimulated indirectly.

RULE 4 Smack to a beat – **whatever groove** gets into your groove. For example, two light smacks followed by one slightly harder smack. Or one light, one hard, two light, one hard and so on.

RULE 5 Stop when whoever is **getting spanked** says it's time to stop.

TIP Asking the person being spanked if she/he will 'be good now' keeps the mood going.

⅄⅄⅄ FREAK OUT LEVEL IF HE WANTS IT AND YOU DON'T

Three Cosmopolitans

You might feel you're with a potential Hannibal Lecter or the Marquis de Sade if he wants to spank you. But if he wants to be spanked, he instantly morphs from stud lover to sad little boy.

Get in touch with your inner dominatrix

Think: your boyfriend has to do exactly what you tell him to, and you don't even have to ask nicely. Sound him out first – to make sure he's up for it. Next time he promises to pick up dinner, say, 'Forget and you're going to have to lick me until I come.' When he arrives home empty-handed, say, **'It's lickin' time.'** If he obliges, you've got a pussy boy on your hands.

Get into the mood.

Find the **fetish object** or objects that get you into femme dom mind-set – a particular pair of thigh-high black leather stiletto boots, a certain lipstick colour, a leather bustier. If you're into rubber dressing, powder or lube your body before climbing into your catsuit. AND rubber doesn't breathe a lot so load up on deodorant as you tend to sweat when you wear it.

Hone your bad-girl persona.

Let the dirty talk rip. **Be masterful.** Call the shots – it makes him feel like you're taking care of him.

Plan your props.

Using a belt, or hitting somebody with your hand or with a crop or flogger – the effect of each one is very different. With **a crop or a cane**, for example, you can hit only on the bum; every other part of the body is too sensitive.

Take the reins,

Once you've got him in on the act, **take control** but don't bully. Push him up against a wall. Press your body against his. Hold his hands back. Press your lips firmly against his and dig in with your tongue. BUT pay attention to how his body responds. If he struggles, stiffens or pulls away, ease up on the *Basic Instinct* vibe (and put that ice pick down, for god's sake). Always listen carefully so you'll know if his oohs become ows.

 FREAK OUT LEVEL IF HE WANTS IT AND YOU DON'T

Three Cosmopolitans

Send this boy home to his mummy.

 **FREAK OUT LEVEL** ON ANY OF THE ABOVE

IF YOU WANT IT AND HE DOESN'T

A pitcher of Cosmopolitans

And a new address. Or you will be forced to continue seeing him forever for fear that he will tell everyone he knows about what you want.

Five things you hope he's not into

- **Golden Showers (doesn't he know what toilets are for?)**
- **Goalie Sex (give it a rest, already)**
- **Navel Lingus (not an erogenous zone!)**
- **Necrophiliac Lays (don't just lie there – do something!)**
- **Dressing in your clothes (that's a pair of Manolo Blahnik's he's eyeing – and you know he'll stretch them)**

THREE'S COMPANY

There is not a man walking this earth who will turn down the opportunity for a threesome. This is **what they dream about**, wish for when they blow out the candles on their birthday cakes and never believe they will have. Be warned, though. Men are generally not Three-ply. Unless your boy is aiming for a PG Rating or Ambisextrous, he'll automatically think, 'Two hot babes in a hot tub' – and so will you. Does this make you a part-time lesbian? Perhaps. But so is three-quarters of the western world. Here are three simple rules for happy threesomes.

1. It should be you who does the choosing.

What's key is whom you choose to share your love juices with. Let him go trolling, and you will forever be suspicious of what he wants in a sex partner (generally, breasts as big as Mont Blanc). Best friends are not ideal for reasons of future jealousy. The same goes for anyone who is much hotter than you. Pick **someone you are attracted to** and who you think will respond. (She's touchy-feely, she's not in a relationship and you know she's horny.)

2. When it happens, go slow.

It works best (emotionally later if not orgasm-wise now) if you and your boyfriend agree that initially everyone is going to **concentrate on you**. You need to be reassured that this is all happening for *your* sexual needs.

3. Don't assume it will be magical.

It won't automatically be an experience in which everyone gets every hole and appendage explored in precisely the way they want it to be. Threesomes are no more effortless than any other kind of sex. In fact, as you increase the number of people, you increase the number of sexual, physical, personality, and other variables. It just gets **more complex**, so accept that, yes, sometimes things will probably be awkward (physically, if in no other way). Three bodies on a bed means that things aren't always going to be graceful.

Threesome turnoffs

When he starts drooling at the mention of a threesome.
You know he's thinking, 'Yippee! Two pussies for the price of one!' Which makes you feel he is a selfish male porcine who doesn't deserve you, let alone see you get it down with another woman.

When the subject comes up and he won't let it go.
Maybe you've been watching a film in which a threesome occurs, or talking about a friend. You'll start worrying: Am I boring in bed? Am I such a bad lay that he needs to double up?

He's jealous of how you feel about the other girl.
That's your job.

Once you do it, he wants to do it all the time.
When you invite a girlfriend over for dinner and he says, winking, 'So how much whipped cream and chocolate sauce should I buy for dessert?' If he is this into it, it makes you wonder what he is doing behind your back.

The meow factor

Don't get catty. There are three points in a triangle and every side is a line drawn between two of those points. That means: you and him, you and her, and him and her. It does not mean: it is you, her and him. It's very rare that all three people are taken into consideration simultaneously, and very common that one person is left out, whether of thoughts or actions, at any given time. This is an award-winning recipe from *How to Screw Up A Threesome Bake-Off*. Deal with it.

CLUBBING

Mile High Club

Book a red-eye flight if possible so that everyone will be too sleepy to notice anything suspicious. To make it official, wait until you reach 1609 m (5,280 ft) AGL – generally cruising altitude – before starting your aerial pleasures. Apparently, the high air pressure makes your orgasm tremendous.

> **OPTION 1** It's easy to hide a **hand job** under one of those little airplane blankets. And if you're really sneaky, you can rest your head on your partner's lap and just happen to have oral sex. Try not to let your head bob up and down.

OPTION 2 Hit the lav. Wait until the film when there's usually no meal or beverage services. Arrive separately (everyone will still guess, but it makes you feel better). Position yourself accordingly. Plane bathrooms are small. The best bet is for him to go in from behind with you bending over the sink or the toilet.

> Investigate Business Class if you don't want cramped bathroom sex. Some airlines have planes equipped with **'fully flat bed'** seats that allow you to get almost completely horizontal. They are arranged in pairs so one person's head is at another person's feet (what could be better?). Just make sure you use the privacy screen.

Swinging clubs

OK, there isn't a person out there who hasn't gotten off on the thought of taking part in an orgy. It's so decadent: all these people just going at it, without a care or conscience. Being the centre of attention, calling the shots, and being pleasured from all angles. **Sexy? Oh, yeah.** But wait – who knows where those genitals have been last night, last week, last year?

- **Rubber** is not always required wear at swing clubs, but very few people will look down on you if you insist.
- You don't have to have sex – you can **just watch** and flirt and make mental notes for what you're going to share with your friends later.

Be aware: it's women who are in high demand at a swing party so this is not a good place to meet men. He can't even get an entrée unless he has a woman on his arm. And your stud may be looked on as a dud. If he's left pouting in the corner while you have a wild time, remember to check in with him from time to time to boost his sagging ego (and other parts).

TIP Ads that ask for money, even discreetly, or which mention 'generosity' are almost certainly from sex workers rather than swingers. In general, you will probably waste less time by placing an ad than by responding to them.

FILL UP YOUR BOX OF TREATS

Vibrators, massage oil, condoms and lube tube – these are the obvious things. But you don't have to break the bank to stock up on **sexy goodies**.

Raid the bathroom

- Rescue those **snagged tights** from the trash bin. They can be used as tie-ups, sensuous hand-job gloves and masks for jump-on-him sex.

- Wrap a **fabric hair band** loosely round his penis and you have yourself a home-made cock ring.

- A dab of minty **toothpaste in your mouth** will give your oral sex a warm tingly sensation.

- A **toothbrush** (preferably new and soft-bristled) can be much sexier than all ten digits and his tongue when pleasuring your love muff.

- **Use a razor** to draw a pretty picture down below. Bonus: no more complaints about short 'n curlies between the teeth.

- **Body cream** makes a sweet substitute for massage oil (as long as you are not following up with rubber).

   TIP Check in any obvious sex toys when travelling. Your nipple clamp will alert security and end up in a big trash bin labelled 'Items Will Not Be Returned'.

Boy toys

Cock rings slip around the base of his penis to restrict blood flow and keep him standing to attention. Most are made of chromed steel or rubber. In fact, most are little more than high-priced gasket rings or chrome-plated circular chain links available at any DIY store. But they have to be chosen carefully, sized for the user.

- A **too-loose** cock ring does nothing.
- A **too-tight** cock ring cuts off all retreating blood flow, thus preventing the cock from ever getting soft. It may sound like fun but can become painful after two hours or so, and may require a trip to Emergency to remove.

Since most guys have an enhanced view of their package, it's better if you do the sizing. Especially because you can then get one that has a built-in **'clit-stimulator'** (doubling your pleasure and fun). But beware: you put yourself at real risk of falling in love with his penis. And, as with most things, there are a few rules to follow when using a cock ring.

1. Don't use one that can't **be removed** easily.
2. Don't leave it on for **more than 20 minutes** at a time.
3. Don't let him **fall asleep** or pass out with it on. Or else his dick might fall off.

WARNING Putting on a solid cock ring can be fiddly – and taking it off can be even fiddlier. He has to be soft to do either, putting first his testicles through the ring, and then his penis. Taking it off is the reverse process, but since one of the purposes of a cock ring is to keep you hard, this can be easier said than done.

Film the act

NUMBER ONE RULE BEFORE THE TAPE ROLLS:

Agree that **you** keep the evidence.

WHY **MAKING YOUR OWN** WINS OVER RENTING

There won't be:

- (hopefully) **ugly male models** with impossibly big dicks and headless women
- **bogus gurus** and ageing sexperts (when was a biology teacher under the sheets erotic?)
- **feeble story lines** featuring one woman with enormous breasts servicing ten enormous penises
- shots of those **extremely large penises** ejaculating (who thought this was pretty?)
- shots of **semen shooting** into women's faces
- **guys thwacking** their wet noodles like fly swatters.

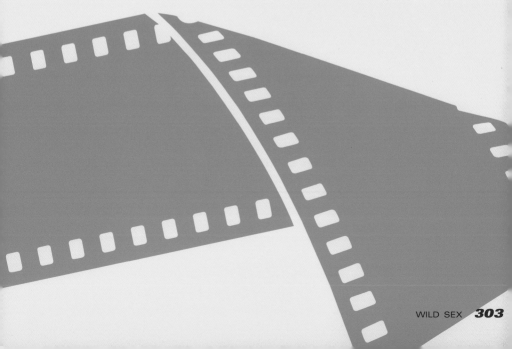

DO THIS **BEFORE YOU START**

1 **Get a fake tan** so you don't need special lighting to make up for your blinding paleness (and you'll be less conscious about the 5 kg (10 lb) the camera is supposed to add).

2 Get a full **body wax**.

3 If the above doesn't include your **love box**, trim your pubic hair.

4 Persuade your man to **shave his scrotum** (tell him it will make him look bigger if he shaves his ball sack and the hair at the base of his penis).

5 Clear the set of unnecessary objects such as tissues, family photographs – **anything that can distract you** when you watch your movie.

6 For the most flattering results, use as much **warm light** as possible (lighting from underneath rather than above).

7 Use **high-quality equipment**. A good tripod will have a quick-release button so you can whip the camera off and move it speedily when needed.

8 Plan to **shoot ten times as much film** as you are going to use – that way you have the freedom to edit out everything that is unflattering.

9 The **position of the camera** is important. Mount it on a tripod (high is better for a good overview), look through the viewfinder and mark off the area in which you will be performing so you don't just film the tops of your heads.

10 **Turn up the heating** – there's nothing less sexy than goose-pimply flesh.

11 Keep at least **one item of clothing** on – stilettos, a camisole – you'll look better than if you are fully naked.

12 **Do some test runs** so he gets used to performing in front of the camera (otherwise he may not rise to the occasion).

13 Smear yourself with **baby oil** to make your skin glisten (but if you're using rubber birth control, make it water).

ONCE THE FILM IS ROLLING

1 **Vary the shots** by moving around as much as possible.

2 Do some **gonzo shots** (porn-speak for when the person holding the camera shows himself off on film).

3 **Don't use the zoom** – it never looks good. Move closer if you have to.

4 Exaggerate your **sound effects** and talk straight to the camera.

5 Use **black and white film** (it is much more flattering).

TIP Check that the film is running – you don't want to find out five hours later as you get ready for replay that you ran out of tape or battery power.

FLATTERING POSITIONS

Bunking Bronco You sit on top, facing away from him. This way the camera sees your boobs bouncing up and down and your face.

Doggy Position the camera so it is pointing up. Keep in mind that if he's directly behind you, then the camera will see only his bottom, so you need to stick yours in the air.

Oral sex His head should be to one side so you can see his tongue darting in and out. He can shoot down when it's his turn (though he might have trouble holding the camera straight).

ONE LAST FABULOUS SUM-IT-UP TIP

Sex is a lot like shopping. The only way you can decide if something works for you is to try it on and wear it for a day.

CHAPTER TEN SEXIONARY OR 'LEARN TO SPEAK THE LANGUAGE OF LOVE'

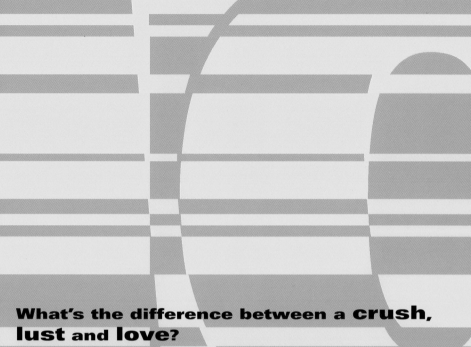

What's the difference between a crush, lust and love?
Spitting, swallowing and gargling.

WHAT DO YOU CALL A MAN WHEN LABELS SUCH AS 'HUNK', 'BABE' OR 'RAT' FAIL TO DESCRIBE HIM? WHAT ABOUT A RELATIONSHIP THAT'S NOT-QUITE CASUAL BUT NOT-QUITE SERIOUS? HERE'S THE SHORTHAND GUIDE TO MODERN LOVE AND ALL THE MEN YOU HAVE KNOWN.

A

Aeroplane Blonde Someone who has blonde hair on top but still has a black box

Alien An artist with a job

Ambisextrous Someone who is bisexual

Amnesia Sex When you think you are having sex with someone new and you realize you two have done the horizontal mamba before

Anal Assailant A person who prefers anal sex

Anticipointment That low-down feeling you get when an event (such as a romp with a gorgeous man) fails to live up to your expectations

Antiquing Dating someone who is much older than you

Assmosis The process by which that potential Mr Right you met at a party turns into a total ass on your first date

B

Bachelor Someone who, when forced to choose, will purchase a super-size can of beer over anything comparable in price

Backed Up A glandular condition (with no medical foundation) from which men believe they suffer when they have not had sex for a long time

Bad Breaker-Upper People who tell the truth to end a relationship

Ball Busters Balls that hang so low they get in the way

Bank Account Someone you are going out with just for the free lunch

Before-Play Any misrepresentation of yourself in order to get laid

Below Zero A sex session that leaves you cold

BHI or Boyfriend Hearing Impairment A condition that occurs when a man who never misses the name of the player up to bat, a word his boss says or the amount of money you spent on shoes suddenly goes deaf when you share a horror story about your boss, some gossip about a friend or say it's time to 'talk about us'.

Bit Flip A sudden 180-degree personality change

Blamestorming Discussing with your boyfriend why some aspect of your relationship isn't working out and who is responsible

Bone of Contention When he has an erection that you did not cause

Born-Again Virgin What you become when you have not had sex for more than six months

Box of Treats Where you keep your vibrator, oil, condoms and lube tube

Boy Friend (as opposed to 'boyfriend') A male who has some flaw which makes sleeping with him totally unappealing

Boy Toy Playing with a man who is at least six years your junior

Breakdown Recovery The friends you call after a break-up

Bulimic Blowjobber Due to a bout with bulimia, someone who has developed the ability to swallow an entire penis in one sitting (of course, they throw it up five minutes later)

Bunny Boiler What you become when a relationship causes you to commit deranged obsessive acts

Buy-sexual 'Buy me something, and I'll be have sex with you.'

C

Calling in a Substitute Dating someone in order to date his friend

Charitable Orgasm You fake it because he is trying so hard and you feel bad for him

Cheating Paradox It's cheating when the other person does it, not when you do it

Childlock Sex You may have to push and screw in order to get relief

Cliterature A selection of one-handed reading material

Code Blue What you call a relationship in trouble

Committing Sexual Perjury Faking it

Computer Man He's hard to figure out and never has enough memory

Contraceptive Dating Avoiding pregnancy by only going out with repulsive men

Crotch Tweaker A guy who can't stop rearranging his family jewels

D

Data Dump When you divulge your ex-boyfriend's sexual quirks, annoying habits and inner secrets to his new girlfriend

Dating Burnout Suffering one-too-many long boring meals and evenings that either end at your front door or with you skulking out of his apartment at 3 am; you can't be bothered to be charming to any more strangers or even work the room at a party

Dating Down When no one can understand what you could possibly see in the person you are dating since you are obviously so much more attractive/successful/interesting/all three than him/her

Dating White-Out The act of doing-over a huge dating mistake

DBA or Don't Bother Asking
What you should do when you spot
a man with a child

Deceptionist Someone who
pretends to have the same priorities,
philosophy, style and enthusiasms
as a potential love partner in order
to hook him/her

Decoy Someone who fills in between
an old relationship and a new one.
She/he seems like the Real Thing, but
is actually just a distraction until the real
Real Thing comes along.

Deja Moo When you're out on a first
date and you get the feeling you've
heard this BS before

Directionally Challenged A lover
who heads straight for your candy store
without stopping at your main course

**Do an RR (Reassess and
Repossess)** The process by which a
dud becomes a stud as soon as you
realize someone else wants him too

Double Bed Dread What you
get when he is about to move into
your space

Double Dipping Dating more than
one person at once

Double Whammy When you
cheat on your boyfriend with his
best friend or he cheats on you
with your best friend

Doucher Someone who is obsessed
with clean sex

Drag King Women, straight or bi,
who dress like men

Drive-By Dumping Ending a
relationship without direct confrontation

E

Earlingus Giving your ear a lick-down

Ego Surfer Someone who constantly
fishes for compliments

E-Male A man who is more
emotionally open online than he
is face-to-face

Er-hem What you call someone when
he isn't your boyfriend and isn't your
long-term lover (and never will be)

Eurocreep A guy of European
descent who has recently come to this
country on a short-term work visa. He
speaks more than one language, rarely
has money, only has models for friends
and most certainly has a wife or
serious girlfriend back home.

F

Fade Out When someone disappears
for a month and then reappears.

Five Pinter Someone you'd only chat
up after you've had a few beers

Fixer Upper A guy who needs work
but is basically in move-in condition

**Double
Dipping**

Flashback Telling your current lover (usually during or just after sex) about your ex – as in, 'My ex-lover could last all day and half the night'

Foreign Market Trolling for love outside your usual hunting grounds

Freelancer Someone who is not interested in a long-term relationship of any kind

Free Market What exists when one of you is caught cheating

The Friends Ploy When one of you says, 'Can we just be friends?' after sex. What the man is really saying is 'Please don't slash my tires' while the woman is really saying 'I want to be friends and forget we had sex at all.'

Fuck Buddy Someone that you get together with only when you are horny

G

The Gap Guy His entire wardrobe consists of khakis with a button-down oxford shirt

Glazing Mastering the technique of sleeping with your eyes open (especially useful for when you are on a snooze date)

Goalie When you have sex, he won't stop until you've come

G-Sport Looking for your G-spot

H

High-Impact Sex High-pressure lovemaking that's hot and hard and comes at high speed

Himbo The male equivalent of a bimbo

Home Bed Advantage That confident feeling you get when having sex in your own environment

I

IBM or Ideal Breeding Material You can envision making babies with this potential partner

IJA or 'I just ate...' Someone who divides the bill to the last penny

IMS or Irritable Male Syndrome His version of PMS

Indecisionitis You can't decide whether to dump the boyfriend or not

J

Julia Roberts Rule When on a date, the person who makes a little money pays for the popcorn and movies while the person who makes a lot pays for the champagne and hotel room

K

Kiss of Death At the end of a date when he kisses you on the nose, chin, cheek, hair – anywhere but your mouth

L

Late Bloomer A man who takes a long time to become erect but when he does... ooh la la!

Law of Kama Sutra Orgasm There are over 2,000 positions – one of them has to work for you

Law of Relativity How attractive your ex appears to be is directly proportionate to how unattractive your date is

Law of the Jungle An all-purpose appeal-proof statute used by men when they have, in any way, behaved badly

Leftover Sex Sex with your ex

Long Distance Relationship An agonizing experience of triple-digit phone bills, too many DIY orgasms by phone sex and constant suspicion regarding the other person's ability not to cheat (based on your own urges)

Lottery Sex A one in a million chance that you'll have an orgasm

Love At First Sight Disorder What occurs when two extremely horny people meet

Love Terrorist Someone who mindlessly destroys the entire foundations of a relationship in one cruel, death blow

Low-Impact sex The slow, sweet kind of lovemaking

M

Maintenance Sex Having sex with someone you've had sex with before but aren't interested in pursuing a long-term relationship with

Male Slut A man good for a quickie – think of him as a shoe that you want to try on but not necessarily buy

M&M Mutual masturbation

Manizer A female with a conquer-all attitude who uses, then loses, men like tissues

Mascara Man He usually runs at the first sign of emotion

Mattressizer Someone who will only have sex in bed

Makeover Queen When you think that with a little effort you can restyle him into the perfect boyfriend

MBD Married But Dating

Millennium Domes Your breasts in a Wonderbra – striking when seen from the outside, but there's nothing worth seeing in there

Mouthing Off Really bad oral sex

N

Natural Selection The scientific explanation for why there are no good ones left past the age of 35

Navel Lingus The art of making love to the belly button

Necrophiliac Lay When your lover just lies there

Nymphomaniac A man's term for a woman who wants to have sex more often than he does

O

Out Yourself When you admit that the only type of sex you've ever had has been missionary

Outie A strap-on vibrator

Oversize Penis A larger-than-average stiffy

P

Part-Time Lesbian A woman who has sex with other women just so she can get the orgasmic benefits

Passing the Sniff Test Having a clean-smelling groin

PDA (Public Displays of Affection) Sex Sex in public

Peer Pressure Sex Sleeping with someone because your friends think he is hot

Petrophobic Someone who is embarrassed to undress in front of a household pet

PG Rating What you give a guy who is probably gay – he is gorgeous, witty, never been in a serious relationship and looks better in your make-up than you

Phonesia The affliction of getting a phone number and then never calling

Pig Pecker Man He comes and then rolls over and plays dead before you're even out of the starting box

Pinocchio Effect Touching your nose when you are telling a lie

Plastic Closet Said about someone who refuses to admit to having cosmetic surgery

The Poppy (Thanksgiving) Effect When your boyfriend breaks up around Remembrance Day or Thanksgiving because it's the pit stop before the Christmas/New Year's romance season

Pre-dating The period of time you spend on the phone and e-mailing before the actual date takes place

Prophet A sensitive New Age type of guy who will cry over the plight of the whales but is dismissive if you get fired

Puppy A guy with Pick Up Potential

Q

Quick Fix What he calls getting in and out of the toilet in under 15 minutes

R

Relationship Karma An ancient Asian belief where how you treat your boyfriend will determine how you are treated by your next boyfriend

Petrophobic

Wedding Controller

Relationship Résumé Putting a positive spin on your previous partners

Re-Run Accidentally running into a one-night-stand lover

Retro-Dating Going out with a guy you previously dated and nixed because you remember him as a lot better than he really is

Retro-Sex Sex where you do it in a bed in missionary position

S

Screen Test What you give each other in the early stages of dating to figure out if the relationship is worth pursuing.

Secret Single Behaviour The bad habits you indulge when you live by yourself

Se-Men Guys who are obsessed with the speed, amount, consistency, taste and shooting force of their ejaculate

Sexual Camel Someone who can go for a long time between acts of sex

A Short Run The length of time one must keep up a relationship after sex (generally two weeks)

Shrinkage His penis experiences this when dipped in cold water

Sixty-Eighter One of you gives the other oral sex with the understanding that the one receiving 'owes' the giver

Size Queen A guy who is obsessed with his penis statistics and hopes he qualifies for an oversize

Soregasm What you get when he wants to do it and you don't

Soul Mate A man you dumped who is now going out with another woman

Speed Shooter Someone who ejaculates in 60 seconds or less

Spill Master Someone who takes control of their own fluids

Step-Ins What you use to get off when he isn't doing it for you

Swiped Out What you are when the guy you are with never has any money, sending you on endless trips to get cash

T

Terror Sex No-contraception sex

Therapeutically Correct Someone who refuses to speak in anything other than the first person and who begins and ends every sentence with what he wants, needs or dislikes, without any room for you to express your desires

Three-ply Someone into threesomes

The Toad Defence What you make after spending money, time and energy to get better acquainted with a person whom you don't especially like in the hope that you will be more attracted to him in the future

Tongue-whipped He's a loser but he gives great oral sex

Trampage What you go on when you sleep with more than one man in a week

Trendoid Well-dressed and confident, his wardrobe will make yours look pathetic by comparison

Trial Marriage First marriage

Trysexual Someone who will try anything at least once

Tweenie A guy who was a nerd as a teenager but is now cool and making up for lost booty time

U

Understudy When you are in a relationship and have a trainee boyfriend waiting in the wings

V

Vagitarian A man who won't perform oral sex

W

Wake-n-Bake A quickie first thing in the morning

Wedding Controller A bride who becomes so controlling she won't allow fat guests in her wedding photos and dresses her bridesmaids in Little Bo-Peep style dresses

WIP or Work In Progress You can see the potential but you'll have to do a lot work before he is ready for the real world

Withdrawal Method Leaving right after a bout of body bumping

Acknowledgements
Many people contributed their knowledge, sense of humour, moral support and witty insight to this book.

Special thanks go to: The Family Planning Association, the Royal College of Obstetricians and Gynaecologists, and Marie Stopes One Call for making sense of contraception and STIs (separately, of course), the Good Vibrations store for insight into the amazing world of erotica and the Kinsey Institute for their weird and wonderful facts on sex. A huge gracias also to all my friends (and hopefully you still are) and those strangers who cheerfully bared their souls and worst and best dating and sex experiences, tips and thoughts.

I would also like to thank my unofficial (and unpaid) researcher, Sy Sussman (who also happens to be a wonderful father) and my official (but also unpaid) babysitter, the fabulous Lorraine Sussman, who dropped everything when the deadline was looming. The usual kisses of gratitude to Steven, Jazz and Tasha.

And, of course, this book would still be an un-named file in my computer without the nurturing of my amazing triple-threat editing team: Zia Mattocks, Judith More and Lisa Dyer. Special thanks also to Mary Davies for her ability to spot an inconsistency at fifty paces and turn my haphazard ramblings into readable language.